ENCOURAGING HETEROSEXUALITY

Helping Children Develop
a Traditional Sexual Orientation

ENCOURAGING HETEROSEXUALITY

Helping Children Develop a Traditional Sexual Orientation

by Douglas A. Abbott, Ph.D.
University of Nebraska

by A. Dean Byrd, Ph.D., MBA, MPH
University of Utah

Millennial Press, Inc.
P.O. Box 1741
Orem, UT 84059

13-DIGIT ISBN: 978-1-932597-66-0
10-Digit ISBN: 1-932597-66-2

Cover design and typesetting by Adam Riggs

Acknowledgments

My parents, Joe and Doris Abbott gave me the opportunity for higher education. The Lord gave me the gift of the gospel of Jesus Christ. Together, a synthesis of science and religion has enabled me to wrestle with this topic and envision this book.

Randy Bott, at Millennial Press, had the faith and courage to publish this manuscript! Because of the tenacity of Dean Byrd, co-author, mentor, counselor, and man of many talents, this project has been completed. Thank you Dean!

Mary, my wife, and best of friends, has kept me going over the past few years of poor health. Thank you for your love and care.

—Douglas A. Abbott, 6 April 2009, Lincoln, Nebraska

I really was not acquainted with Doug before this joint venture. How quickly I learned that we both shared the same view the Gospel of Jesus Christ: it embraces all truth whether it comes from the scientific laboratory or the revealed word of God.

I am indebted to a Southern Baptist father and a Chinese Buddhist mother who taught me that truth was discovered, not constructed. And a wife, Elaine and wonderful children, whose support has always been unwavering

It has been incredible working with my co-author Doug—he is so much like a kindred spirit. And Randy Bott—his willingness to stand up for truth is so refreshing.

And finally, to the children many of whom we will never know, whose lives just might be impacted by something I had a part in writing, I am grateful for the blessing they are in our lives.

—A. Dean Byrd, 6 April 2009, Salt Lake City, Utah

TABLE OF CONTENTS

FOREWORD

The purpose of this book is to present a case for encouraging hetero-sexuality in children without taking a negative approach toward those who engage in homosexual behavior or those who champion gay rights. This is not an easy task. We are both trained psychologists, and Christians, which leaves us at odds (on certain issues) with the majority of the scientific community of psychologists, psychiatrists, social workers, and marriage and family therapists.

In this manuscript we take an unorthodox approach and combine secular, scientific information with our personal religious beliefs. Judged by academics, this is an inappropriate endeavor because science is objective and has truth value while religion is subjective and idiosyncratic. We accept scientific findings, although all research has inherent flaws and limitations--and is often misinterpreted. In this book we reference over 270 scientific journal articles, academic books, and scholarly on-line resources. Our interpretation of secular research, however, is tempered by spiritual truth revealed by God.

Yet, most social scientists stubbornly reject the possibility of revealed truth. For these professionals, knowledge about human nature and human behavior comes only from applying the scientific method. One must do research and record behavior, using valid and reliable instruments, and then test hypotheses using statistics. It is assumed that if you can't observe and measure it, it doesn't exist. Thus, the influence of God and His Spirit of Light and Truth is immaterial because its presence cannot be established scientifically. Obviously, we take issue with this assumption.

Neal A. Maxwell (1926-2004), church leader, encouraged behavioral scientists who are Christian to build bridges between God's revealed truth and the world of secular science.[1] He believed it was possible to "*listen with the ears of scholarship and scripture*", and by so doing, one could come to a more complete and accurate understanding of human nature and behavior. However, Elder Maxwell warned that attempts to "converge scientific facts with scriptural truths" may engender scorn and reproof from the academic community. But bridge building must be attempted even if one's efforts are seen as "*stumbling blocks*" to some and "*foolishness*" to others.[2]

We believe that a competent scholar and a good Christian can coexist in the halls of higher learning, though at times, uncomfortably. One with dual citizenship, in academia and in God's gospel flock, can seek truth in secular science, but can also get added insights from revealed truth. Paul the Apostle gives good counsel to the Christian scientist when he said: "*We should not conform to worldly wisdom, but we should be transformed by God's Spirit which will renew and enlighten our minds to establish that which is good, acceptable, and perfect in Christ*".[3]

We reiterate our belief that God can reveal truth about human nature and behavior undiscovered by the scientific method. Saint Paul taught the disciples of Jesus that knowledge can be given by God's spirit, the Holy Ghost:

> Which things also we speak, not in the words which man's wisdom teaches, but which the Holy Ghost teaches; [discerning] spiritual things with spiritual [eyes].
> *But the natural man receives not the things of the Spirit of God: for they are foolishness unto him: neither can he know them, because they are spiritually discerned.*[4]

In one sense, the "natural man" is anyone who relies solely on personal learning and experience, the judgment and opinions of others, and the scientific method to provide all truth and knowledge. A Christian prophet spoke of those who are wise in their own sight and reject revealed truth:

> "O the vainness, and the frailties, and the foolishness of men! When they are learned they think they are wise, and they hearken not unto the counsel of God, for they set it aside, supposing they know of themselves, wherefore, their wisdom is foolishness and it profit them not."[5]

C. S. Lewis (1898-1963, Irish novelist and lay theologian) suggested that man-without-God (i.e., one who lives by worldly wisdom but lacks divine truth) is destined to fail in his study of human nature. Lewis recommends that the wise and prudent person will always consider God in his calculations.

> "The moment you have a self at all, there is a possibility of putting yourself first—wanting to be the centre—wanting to be God, in fact. That was the sin of Satan: and that was the sin he taught the human race. Some people think the fall of man had something to do with sex, but that is a mistake. . . . What Satan put into the heads of our remote ancestors was the idea that they could 'be like gods'— could set up on their own as if they had created themselves—be their own masters—invent some sort of happiness for themselves outside God, apart from God. And out of that hopeless attempt has come . . . the long terrible story of man trying to find something other than God which will make him happy."[6]

The saddest statement in all of Holy Writ is a short verse about an ancient people, who were once enlightened by Christ, but over time they fell into disbelief and sin. *"For behold, the Spirit of the Lord hath already ceased to strive with [them]; and they are without Christ and God in the world; and they are driven about as chaff before the wind [of worldly wisdom].*[7] Paul made a similar observation that men would be "aliens" to Christ and estranged from God's promise of eternal life *"having no hope, without God in the world."*[8] If we only accept scientific knowledge and ignore divine truth we will be as Paul said, *"ever learning, but never able to come to the knowledge of [the full] truth."*[9]

As Christians we are well-aware of Christ's injunction: *"Judge not, that ye be not judged."*[10] Some interpret this to mean you can never judge anyone for anything! What an absurd circumvention! Without *judgment* on personal and interpersonal behaviors (i.e., a determination of right or wrong, good or bad, healthy or unhealthy) a society will devolve into selfishness, brutality, and moral chaos. For example, a husband may believe he can beat his wife when she is uncooperative and disagreeable. Yet, we *judge* his behavior to be wrong and immoral.

As you read this book you may surmise that the authors are judging something they should not: adult, consensual, sexual behavior. This is not the case! We judge no man or woman, let them do as they please; yet on moral issues that affect society, judgments must be made. One should realize that sexual behavior is not a private matter but a public health concern because it can adversely affect so many others, often innocent children.

Christ adjudicated the woman found guilty of adultery, a serious social issue.[11] Jesus disapproved of the harsh treatment of stoning her to death, but he upheld and sustained the Jewish judgment that adultery is an immoral action and requires remorse and repentance. He told the woman, with compassion but resoluteness, "Go and sin no more.", or in other words, "You may leave without punishment, but you must stop this behavior, it is wrong and destructive to yourself, your family, and to your community." The Ten Commandments given to Moses are judgments on human thought, intension, and behavior, five of which are incorporated into the civil laws of almost every country.[12] Moral judgments are a requisite of any civil society.

In sum, we readily acknowledge that a portion of American adults would disagree with our position, some strongly. Many Americans believe that homosexuality is a legitimate form of sexual expression, or at least that it is a benign behavior without negative consequences for individuals or society. We disagree. Our least critical opponents will accuse us of intolerance. The most critical will call us homophobic (a misused and misunderstood term). Our right to disagree, however, should be accepted without animosity from our academic peers or personal attacks from critics. All people should be treated with kindness, tolerance and with respect for diverse opinions! We make our case, hopefully, without rancor or ill will toward those who believe otherwise. We urge readers to judge our position on its merits and come to their own conclusions.

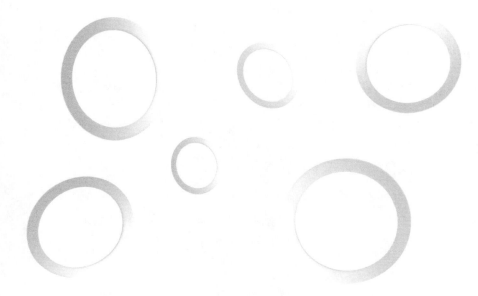

"In American society, everything is tolerated
except those who do not tolerate everything."

—Anonymous

CHAPTER ONE
INTRODUCTION

For centuries Christians, Jews, and Muslims (about half the world's population) have believed that certain actions and behaviors are forbidden by God.[1] Theft, murder, and dishonoring parents are examples of behaviors religious believers condemn and find morally wrong. These religious believers have also maintained the tradition that sex outside of marriage is prohibited and that heterosexual marriage is the ideal adult relationship.[2] Recently, beliefs in traditional marriage and sexual expression have been seriously challenged in western societies.[3] Within the last forty years, time-honored religious standards regarding sexuality have been abandoned by a large proportion of American and European societies.[4] Educators, psychologists, psychiatrists, and even religious leaders have questioned long-established beliefs in chastity, fidelity, and heterosexuality.[5]

The 2000 census data indicated that there are at least 600,000 homosexual households in America, about half lesbian and half gay, representing a 314% increase just since the 1990 census.[6] About one-third of these homosexual couples have children in the home. Undoubtedly, there are more lesbian and gay couples and individuals not reported in official statistics.[7] Thus, because of the size of the gay community and the activist efforts of its leaders, homosexuality has become an important social, political, and family issue.[8]

Today, some people believe that homosexuality is a natural, normal variation of human sexual expression, not so unlike right or left handedness.[9] Homosexual marriage is now legal in five US states. Homosexual domestic partnerships are recognized in many US cities and in a few states;

homosexual adoption is legal in some states.[10] The American Associations of Psychiatry, Psychology, Social Work, Medicine, and Pediatrics all endorse homosexual behavior as a non-pathological alternative to heterosexuality.[11]

Even some Jews and Christians accept the legitimacy of homosexuality.[12] For example, both Yip and White consider homosexuality one of God's creations and a deliberate act of divine will.[13] They reject traditional religious doctrine and scripture that condemn homosexual behavior and consider them outdated or misinterpreted. These authors believe that the men of Sodom (a story in the Hebrew Bible) were destroyed not for homosexual rape (as traditionally understood) but rather for being selfish and inhospitable.

Despite the widespread tolerance of homosexuality in America, many people believe that heterosexuality is preferable.[14] About half of American adults believe that homosexual behavior is wrong, unnatural, or immoral.[15] Most Americans, however, also believe that homosexuals should not be subjected to any kind of harassment, discrimination, or punishment.[16] Almost all Americans believe that hate speech and violence against homosexuals is deplorable and unacceptable.[17] Furthermore, we are saddened by those few in our society who sponsor hate or violence against homosexuals or any other group. We do not support any attempt to coerce homosexuals to become heterosexuals; yet we endorse the right of those dissatisfied with their sexual orientation to seek help. Tolerance and ethicality are indeed two-way streets.

Even with an attitude of tolerance, many Americans still oppose the general social acceptance of homosexual behavior and want their children to be heterosexual. But the encouragement of heterosexuality (in private or in public) is difficult to do without upsetting someone. When attempted, disparaging labels soon follow: bigot, blockhead, homophobe.[18] In our politically correct society, it appears impossible to make a positive case for heterosexuality without offending self-identified homosexuals.[19] Yet, it is our contention that heterosexuality can be encouraged in our homes, churches, and communities without hurting or necessarily offending those who promote homosexuality. We realize that some offense cannot be avoided, because if we argue a case for heterosexuality, by simple inference homosexual behavior would be seen as somehow deviant or deficient.

We want to be clear that our preference for heterosexuality "is not an argument for intolerance, bigotry, or lack of compassion" for those who engage in homosexual activity.[20] Tolerance should be central to all our discussions. However, like most virtues, tolerance pressed to its extreme may become a vice. A Christian church leader, Dallin H. Oaks, observed, "Love and tolerance are incomplete unless they are accompanied by a concern for truth."[21] He further noted that "carried to an undisciplined excess, love and tolerance can produce indifference to truth and justice, and opposition to unity."[22] Emphasizing the same point, another church leader, Boyd K. Packer, concluded, "The word *tolerance* is invoked as though it overrules everything else. Tolerance may be a virtue, but it is not *the* commanding one. There is a difference between what one is and what one does. What one is may deserve unlimited tolerance; what one does, only a measured amount. A virtue when pressed to the extreme may turn into a vice."[23]

Our Purpose and a Preview of this Book

Our thesis revolves around the concept of "sexual orientation". This refers to one's consistent and persistent desire for sexual gratification (expressed through actions, fantasies, and self-labeling) with members of the opposite sex (heterosexuality), with someone of the same sex (homosexuality), or with either sex (bisexuality). We present three controversial propositions. First, we posit that heterosexuality is innate and natural and that heterosexuality is the most healthy and functional sexual orientation. Second, we propose that one's sexual orientation can be fostered and encouraged early in development to strengthen a child's heterosexual potential. Third, we believe that if something goes awry in the person's psychological-social-biological environment and he or she engages in homosexual behavior, that person can return to a heterosexual orientation.

The term "sexual orientation" is used by all mental health professionals because it implies a biological predestination—i.e., that genetics and hormones determine sexual orientation. We prefer to use the term "sexual preference" because it suggests both choice and the possibility of change. Also, sexual preference does not rule out the influence of other factors in shaping one's sexual orientation.

In the chapters that follow, we present our case using scientific information *and* religious doctrine. It is our belief that one cannot understand or evaluate complex human behaviors such as sexual preference using science alone. Empirical data can never settle the question of whether a behavior is right or wrong, good or bad, moral or immoral. This requires a value judgment, and a judgment requires a moral value system.

Religion is a source of truth for most of the world's population. For example, "Thou shall not kill (murder)," "Thou shall not commit adultery," "Thou shall not bear false witness" are religious beliefs that influence secular laws and social customs worldwide. Such beliefs are considered true principles but have no support from the secular, scientific realm. Integrating religious belief and scientific knowledge is quite common in many aspects of family life including parenting practices, mate selection, marital relationships, and birth and death rituals. The reader can judge whether our synthesis of science and religion is legitimate and convincing or not.

It is interesting that LeVay and Hamer, both self-identified homosexuals, make our same argument. LeVay states, "First, science itself cannot render judgments about human worth or about what constitutes normality or disease. These are value judgments that individuals must make for themselves, while taking scientific findings into account."[24] Hamer concludes, "Biology is amoral; it offers no help in distinguishing between right and wrong. Only people guided by their values and beliefs can decide what is moral and what is not."[25]

In Chapter 2, we present the assumptions upon which our thesis is built. Assumptions are general statements taken to be true, for the sake of argument, but cannot be scientifically tested. In addition, basic concepts relating to heterosexuality and homosexuality are defined. Understanding these concepts will allow the reader to better comprehend the scientific information presented in Chapter 3.

In Chapter 3, extant theories (i.e., general explanations of homosexuality) are presented and critiqued. Theories are important in science because they provide explanations for why we behave as we do. In this case, if you want to *increase* a child's heterosexual potential and *decrease* the likelihood of homosexuality, you would need to understand the causes of homosexual attraction and behavior. This assumes there are environmental influences, and it's not all innate (i.e., genetic). If you understand what causes a thing to happen, you can then attempt to influence those causes and alter the outcome.

In Chapter 4, we challenge the dominant explanation of homosexuality--that homosexual behavior is innate (i.e., genetic). We present evidence and arguments that human agency (free will and choice) plays an important role in homosexual behavior.

In Chapter 5, we present our theory of homosexuality that combines biological predispositions, environmental factors and moral agency.

In Chapter 6, our theoretical model of homosexuality is used to elucidate practical advice for parents, clergy, and others who seek to support a heterosexual preference in children.

Chapter 7 is a brief conclusion where we acknowledge the limitations of our thesis. We admit we don't have all the answers, and that our perspective is, after all, only our interpretation of the scientific data and the application of our personal religious beliefs.

CHAPTER TWO
ASSUMPTIONS AND CONCEPTS

Assumptions are general statements of belief considered to be true. They cannot be tested and proven. They are simply taken for granted for the sake of discussion.[1] Our assumptions act as a lens through which we evaluate and interpret scientific information and integrate religious belief. Our worldview is influenced by Christian theology, but our view is no different in principle from worldviews adopted by psychologists, psychiatrists, marriage and family therapists, social workers, or educators. These men and women also have foundational worldviews but are usually unwilling or incapable of expressing them openly. Their worldviews, like ours, are empirically untestable.

Worldviews are comprised of ideas, principles, and assumptions believed to be true in the natural world. For example, many psychologists base their theories and treatments on secular humanism and the theory of Darwinian evolution. Secular humanists believe that the physical world (nature) is all that is real. As such, this theory emphasizes scientific inquiry, rejects revealed knowledge (i.e., God and spiritual revelation), and disclaims any type of theistic morality (i.e., God-given moral laws). Secular humanists believe that the universe has been randomly created and that humanity exists without purpose or design. Humankind is a part of nature and has emerged as a result of continuous, natural, evolutionary forces (Darwinism). We are simply animals with bigger brains and some type of self-awareness. Personal fulfillment, individual growth, and personal autonomy are the primary concerns of humankind. In short, though social justice is the goal of secular humanism, there is no higher purpose than personal pleasure.

This brief digression into worldviews is presented so that the reader will understand that all people—including scientists, mental health professionals, and educators—have overarching worldviews that guide their theories and direct their interventions into the physical and psychological realms of human life. Our worldview, which includes Christian ideas and principles, is no less legitimate than theirs; it's just different! It should be accepted on equal footing with other major worldviews. Our Christian viewpoint is one of many, but it is not an illegitimate stepchild to the nonreligious or secular worldviews that dominate psychology, education, and mental health.

Assumptions

Our thesis—that a heterosexual orientation should be preferred and encouraged—is built upon five assumptions. First, we believe there is something beyond our senses: something out of reach of the scientific method.[2] We live not just in the material world, but in a spiritual world where God exists and reigns over all humanity. It is through our connection to God— most often seen in some form of religious belief and practice—that we may obtain some kinds of knowledge and truth independent of the scientific and material world. Thomas and Rogharr concur that "there are [spiritual] realities that exist independent of us that can be known and that these realities do have some generalizing properties, principles that very likely hold across time and space."[3]

In the scriptural writings of Jews, Christians, and Muslims, God created male and female and commanded them to marry and have children. Jesus taught that a man should leave his parents and be joined to his wife in unity and harmony.[4] In our opinion, nowhere in any of the sacred writings of these three major religions does God permit, condone, or encourage homosexual unions; however, there are those who disagree with our assessment.[5] Dailey supports our view: "Scripture reveals the divine design for human sexuality ... Human fullness is to be found in the male and female complementarily ... While many [heterosexual] marriages admittedly fall short of this ideal, homosexual unions are intrinsically flawed and cannot hope to emulate the deep bond that can only occur within a marriage between a man and a woman."[6]

For us personally, it is through inspiration (i.e., revelation) from God that we know our divine natures to be heterosexual, that men and women are equal yet different, and that their union and complementary natures can

google functional
medicine
Board cert, mD
wholistic
doctor

lead to a life of joy, peace, and happiness. Personal revelation as a source of truth, however, is rejected by science because it cannot to observed, measured, and empirically tested. It is clear that "science has no place for revelation as a source of knowledge."[7]

Our second assumption is that heterosexuality is the innate design for humankind. It is an automatic default program for humans, unless something interferes with its expression. In other words, heterosexuality *is not primarily a learned behavior* but is part of our spiritual and genetic makeup. Of course, environment can shape its expression and can aid or hinder its development, but it develops quite naturally on its own—innately and automatically.

On the other hand, homosexuality is primarily a learned behavior (though this learning may not be totally conscious, not so unlike learning that takes place in attraction, sexual or otherwise) and is not solely determined by genes and biology. There may be biological predispositions (i.e., precursors) such as certain personality traits that may lead to homosexual behavior in some individuals, but environment plays the key role. A predisposition is not a direct, determining cause. The notion often heard is that heterosexuality and homosexuality are on a continuum, with heterosexuality and homosexuality on opposite sides. But our view is that we are spiritual, heterosexual beings and that homosexuality represents a deviation from heterosexuality, not the opposite of heterosexuality. This idea may be reached whether you believe in a creator's divine design or the impersonal theory of evolution: both conclude that homosexuality is a deviation and is maladaptive to species survival.

The reason we believe that homosexual behavior is primarily learned is that God would not predetermine an individual to be homosexual if that behavior stood in opposition to God's divine plan for heterosexual family life. It is incompatible with our theological beliefs that God, working through biological processes, would doom any individual to failure in this very important aspect of life. Howard, an ex-lesbian, echoes this feeling: "God wouldn't create us with homosexual thoughts and desires, and then turn around and condemn us for having them! That's not within the character of a just God."[8] In Chapter 3, we present a detailed discussion of how emotional conditioning, learning, and agency may interact to produce a homosexual outcome.

Our third assumption is that homosexual behavior is not a mental illness but an adaptation that involves moral choice. There may be predispositions to such behavior, but behavior by definition is what a person does. A mental illness is a severe emotional or thought disturbance that unfavorably affects a person's interpersonal relationships, health, or safety.[9] The married person who commits adultery, the college student who engages in premarital sex, or the middle-aged man who participates in homosexual behavior are not suffering from mental illnesses. Their actions are immoral because they operate in opposition to the fidelity of a monogamous, heterosexual marriage—God's gold standard for intimate human relationships.

Fourth, we believe that widespread social acceptance of homosexuality will undermine the viability and desirability of the two-parent, heterosexual family.[10] Since the 1970s many people have argued that all family forms are equally good (i.e., healthy, functional, nurturing), and that there was no advantage for a child to have a biological, two-parent family. But this view has been discredited by the huge amount of social-scientific data that demonstrate that, in general, a child reared in a heterosexual, two-parent family does better emotionally, socially, and academically than the average child raised in other types of families.[11]

Our fifth and last assumption is the most controversial and the one most likely to upset and offend those who disagree with us. We believe that the widespread acceptance and legal recognition of homosexual behavior will lead to the exploitation of children by adults. As homosexuality is integrated into our society, adult-child sex will become more common. For some individuals, sex with minors is not always considered harmful and abusive. In fact, in her book *Harmful to Minors*, published by the University of Minnesota Press, Judith Levine suggested that children should not be protected from sex with adults. Levine concludes that sex between children and adults isn't a bad thing if it's done right, that children should be allowed to consent to sex with adults and with each other. Levine states: "Teens often seek out sex with older people, and they do so for understandable reasons: an older person makes them feel sexy and grown up, protected and special; often the sex is better than it would be with a peer who has as little skill as they do."[12]

Numerous academics also support Levine's position that child-adult sex is not inherently wrong.[13] Though most gays and lesbians will not openly condone sex with children, there is nevertheless an "intersection of common ground" between the gay rights agenda and efforts of some gays and lesbians to decriminalize "consensual" sex between adults and adolescents.[14] There are those in the mental health professions who argue that pedophilia (an adult who is sexually attracted to children) should not be considered a mental disorder. Psychiatrist Charles Moser, of San Francisco's Institute for the Advanced Study of Human Sexuality, and co-author Peggy Kleinplatz argued that people whose sexual interests are atypical, culturally forbidden, or religiously proscribed should not, for those reasons, be labeled mentally ill.[15]

In the December 2002 issue of the *Archives of Sexual Behavior*, prominent mental health experts argued in favor of de-pathologizing pedophilia. One author (Green) compares the debate to the declassifying of homosexuality as a mental disorder, and another (Schmidt) offers the following view: "The dilemma is tragic because the pedophile's sexual orientation is deeply rooted in the basic structure of his identity. Pedophilia is as much a part of him as is love for the same or opposite sex for the homosexual or heterosexual man or woman, the difference being that the one is accepted, while the other is categorically forbidden and virtually impossible to realize. In view of the pedophile's burden, the necessity of denying himself the experience of love and sexuality, he deserves respect rather than contempt."[16]

Baldwin asserts that the "homosexual culture commonly promotes sex with children ... [and] targets children both for their own sexual pleasure and to enlarge the homosexual movement."[17] Schmidt declared that gays yearn for any-and-all sexual behavior to be permissible "if it is experienced positively" and does not harm anyone.[18] Constantine readily confessed that "we tread, *small step by small step*, toward healthier acceptance of the sexuality for all, young and old" (our emphasis).[19] Constantine further asserts that if sex between adults and children is "mutual and voluntary," then "not all sexual contact between adults and children can be categorically dismissed as abuse."[20] Constantine claims that "there is a strong probability that the child will not be harmed, and may even benefit" from adult-child sex.[21]

There are efforts in many countries (including the US) to lower the age of sexual consent so that adolescents can have "consensual" sex with adults; then adults will not be punished for statutory rape or child abuse.[22] The age of consent for heterosexual or homosexual sex is 12 years of age in the Netherlands, 13 in Spain and South Korea, 14 in Italy and Austria, and 15 in France. In the state of New Mexico, for example, children as young as 13 may consent to homosexual sex. Gay men will publicly claim that "the molestation of boys is not part of the homosexual lifestyle ... [but] on the other [hand] they are quietly establishing the legal parameters exempting the molestation of boys from prosecution on anti-discrimination grounds."[23]

Most Americans assume that pedophiles are mostly men who prey upon female children, but 25% of pedophiles are men who molest underage boys.[24] "Despite the efforts of homosexual activists to distance the gay lifestyle from pedophilia, there remains a disturbing connection between the two … A disproportionate number of gay men seek adolescent males or boys as sexual partners."[25]

Supporters of this perverse agenda have introduced the term "intergenerational intimacy" or "adult-child sex" to replace the value-laden term *pedophilia* so the behavior sounds less objectionable. They define pedophilia as coercive sex *only* with prepubescent children.[26] As Rind et al., declared, "A willing [pedophilic] encounter with positive reactions would be labeled simply, *adult-child sex*, a value neutral term."[27] Brongersma is even more outspoken and asserts that a "loving pedophile" can give the kind of "companionship, security, and protection which parents and peers cannot give."[28] Jones asserts that "homosexual intergenerational intimacy may be developmentally functional."[29] The term "developmentally functional" means healthy, appropriate, and good for children!

Admittedly, this fifth assumption—that societal acceptance of homosexuality will increase the sexual exploitation of children—lacks direct empirical support. But the lack of direct proof does not, by itself, disqualify our hypothesis that integration of homosexuality into American culture will increase the sexual abuse of children. An untested hypothesis still remains a possibility. Numerous authors indicate that there is a connection between gay rights and the clandestine push to legalize adult-adolescent sex. For example, Baldwin describes in detail how *some* homosexual leaders; many mainstream gay newspapers, magazines, and websites; and even professional journals (e.g., *Journal of Homosexuality, Journal of Sex Research*, and *Archives of Sexual Behavior*), sanction sex between adults and adolescents.[30] Thus, it is our firm belief that our society's general acceptance of homosexuality will, in the end, further erode social disapproval of sex between adults and children. Holloway concluded "that the sexual liberation of adults [both heterosexuals and homosexuals] leads inevitably, if unintentionally, to the sexual exploitation of children."[31]

In summary, our assumptions must be accepted or dismissed as they stand. We cannot take more time and space to explain or defend them. Some readers will reject our religious assumptions as illegitimate and unscientific. Those who do, however, should realize that many gay scientists and gay mental health professionals base their research and writing on values derived from secular humanism, moral liberalism, modern essentialism, or some other autonomy-based ethical system.[32] These theories bias those who hold them, just as Christian ideology biases Christian social scientists. Bias is unavoidable.

Bias, however, is not a "four-letter" word—it's not a profane or vulgar term. It simply means a preference for one thing over another.[33] We all have biases: for cats or dogs, for Italian or Chinese food, for hard-rock music or classical symphony. Bias is inherent in our being. Biases are simply the presuppositions upon which to build a thesis. All theories have fundamental assumptions (biases); but in many cases the author's biases are hidden and covert. We hope the reader can use our self-revelation to better judge the merits of our position.

Definitions of Key Concepts

In order to understand our position, it is important to define terms that will be used in this paper. *Homo* is the Latin word for "same," and *hetero* is derived from a Greek word meaning "different."[34] *Gay* or *homosexual* can refer to either male or female homosexuals but usually describes men. A female homosexual is a lesbian. An *ex-gay* is someone who has stopped homosexual behavior and (a) lives a celibate life because he or she has not yet made a comfortable connection to heterosexuality, or (b) lives a normal heterosexual life.[35] It is important to note that some ex-gays have diminished their homosexual attraction and stopped their unwanted homosexual behavior.[36] Many social scientists and laypersons believe there is no such thing as an ex-gay. In their minds, an ex-gay person never was really gay to begin with, or the person is only suppressing his or her natural homosexual desire and only appears temporarily to be heterosexual.

HOMOSEXUAL

Homosexual refers to being emotionally and erotically attracted to members of one's own sex. *Gay* is a term that is used synonymously with *homosexual* (though some consider *gay* to be a social, political identity—a desire to be identified as a practicing homosexual). The gay man or lesbian woman fantasizes about, and engages in, intimate sexual behaviors with someone of the same sex. Homosexual identities, however, are more complex than just sexual behavior and involve emotional, social, and political aspects. "Homosexuality is not a unitary phenomenon, but rather represents a variety of ... overt behaviors and psychological experiences."[37] A detailed discussion of the variations in homosexuality can be found in Murray and Golden.[38]

Some authors who oppose social acceptance of homosexuality refuse to use the term homosexual as a noun because it implies a condition that is innate and immutable.[39] They suggest that homosexual should only be used as an adjective, such as in *homosexual behavior* or *homosexual identity*. Medinger suggests that the word homosexuality describes a "person's feelings or behavior, but not who he or she is."[40] Oaks concludes that "the words homosexual, lesbian and gay are adjectives to describe particular thoughts, feelings or behaviors. We should refrain from using these words as nouns to identify particular conditions or specific persons ... because this implies that a person is consigned by birth to a circumstance in which he or she has no choice in respect to the critically important matter of sexual behavior."[41]

Gay activists proclaim that as much as 10% to 25% of the adult population is homosexual. These exaggerated estimates are circulated in popular culture to suggest that since so many are gay, it must be normal. Gay activists also point out that homosexuality has been found in almost every culture throughout time, and in some animal species, so it must be natural. But the same could be said of many deviant behaviors such as incest. Best estimates based on large, representative samples put the figure much lower. Only 1 to 2% of women self-identify as exclusively homosexual and only 3 to 5% of men self-identify as exclusively homosexual.[42]

HOMOPHOBIA

In common usage, homophobia means an irrational fear, dislike, or loathing of homosexuals.[43] The word *irrational* implies lack of reason, without mental clarity or sound judgment. Homophobia is a pejorative term and connotes action: discrimination, harassment, or even violence. Greenberg and associates assume that homophobes fear their own potential for homosexuality, and so lash out to protect themselves.[44] Homophobia is believed to exist due to ignorance (of the biogenetic causes of homosexuality), bigotry, and old-fashioned religious prejudice.[45]

There are certainly a few "homophobes" in our society, but we believe the label "homophobia" is inappropriate for the great majority of people who oppose homosexuality. Strictly speaking, a phobia is an irrational fear of an object (or situation), which fear interferes with a person's psychological or social functioning.[46] Many who oppose social acceptance of homosexuality do so *without* fear or hate and base their opposition on what they consider to be logical reasons. As O'Donohue and Caselles point out, "It is not irrational for an individual who believes that an act is immoral to want to avoid people who act in such a manner."[47] Such people do not seek to harm anyone or take away a person's civil rights because of sexual behavior. These people are not homophobes, but refuse to accept homosexual behavior on religious and moral grounds.

HETEROSEXISM

In some writings heterosexism replaces the label homophobia and has been defined as an "ideological system that denies, denigrates, and stig-matizes any non-heterosexual form of behavior, identity, relationship, or community."[48] Proponents claim that this concept is similar to other forms of prejudice including racism, sexism, and ageism. Heterosexism includes negative attitudes and behaviors toward gay men and lesbians. In the most common contexts heterosexism is used interchangeably with homophobia, while some writers only use the term homophobia to describe the negative attitudes and hostile emotions that homosexual individuals hold toward themselves.[49]

SEX AND GENDER

Many professionals and members of the lay public have confused the terms sex and gender and tend to use the two terms interchangeably. Sex refers to biological sex—whether a person is male or female based on genes and genitals. However, gender refers to what it means to be male or female. Many self-identified gays and lesbians report no confusion about whether they are male or female. Rather, the difficulties emerge in what it means to be male of female. This is a gender identity issue.

SEXUAL ORIENTATION

This concept refers to one's consistent and persistent desire for sexual gratification (expressed through actions and/or thoughts) with members of the opposite sex (heterosexuality), with someone of the same sex (homo-sexuality), or with either sex (bisexuality).[50] Sexual orientation is thought to be solidified during the adolescent years.[51] Most scholars, however, do not accept a one-dimensional view of sexual orientation. "Any definition based solely on behavior is bound to be deficient and misleading."[52]

Most scientists favor a complex, multi-faceted theory that sexual orientation includes (a) sexual behavior, (b) sexual desires or behavioral intentions, (c) mental fantasies about sex, (d) emotional attachments for men or women, and (e) one's self-identified sexual preference.[53] Some authors suggest that these aspects of sexual orientation are fluid and may change over time. Sexual orientation is the preferred term in the medical and psychological communities because it implies a genetic basis for homosexual behavior.

SEXUAL PREFERENCE

This concept refers to the object of one's sexual desires, fantasies, and behaviors. Some people prefer sex with either males or females, and some with only one sex. If one believes that homosexual behavior is primarily learned, and is chosen, then sexual preference is a more appropriate term than sexual orientation. The phrase "sexual orientation" implies a set of innate (biologically based) personality traits, while "sexual preference" indicates active choice and changeability. Most mental health professionals reject the term sexual preference because it implies choice.

SEXUAL PREFERENCE UNCERTAINTY (A NEW CONCEPT)

This is our term for an individual who has some questions or concerns about the object of his or her sexual desires. The person is unsure whether he or she is attracted to members of his or her own sex, to the opposite sex, or to both sexes. Those with sexual preference uncertainty often believe in many misconceptions about human sexuality, gender identity, and gender role behaviors. This term, unfortunately, is not used in the scientific literature because most academics and mental health professionals believe that any heterosexual who feels confused about sexual preference is really a latent homosexual or bisexual and that the issue is sexual orientation, not sexual preference.

GENDER IDENTITY

Gender identity refers to the emotional and mental sense of maleness or femaleness. It is one's subjective sense of being a man or a woman that is usually well-formed by age three.[54] Many self-identified gays and lesbians, according to some scientists, report a "normal" sense of gender identity. They report being comfortable and content to be male or female, but they desire physical intimacy with members of their own sex. Gender identity sets the stage for sexual preference (orientation) and gender identity can be influenced by parents, peers, the media, and other aspects of the culture. If children grow up with a firm sense of being male or female they will likely choose a traditional sexual preference.

GENDER IDENTITY CONFUSION

This concept refers to a mild-to-moderate feeling of anxiety or unhappiness with one's assigned gender and gender roles. The person does not completely reject his or her sex, but at times wishes he could be a girl or she could be a boy. This experience is not uncommon in the early years of life but does not necessarily indicate the child will suffer later from Gender Identity disorder. Such children may develop a more androgynous lifestyle and be quite content to be male or female. Or for some children this simply becomes a period of transition.

GENDER IDENTITY DISORDER

This refers to a profound, deep-seated dissatisfaction with one's sex and gender.[55] This individual feels a strong and persistent desire that he or she is of the other sex.[56] The person would prefer the identity and the social roles of the opposite sex. For example, a person with XY chromosomes and male genitalia could believe he was really a woman trapped inside a man's body. He would have a female gender identity and would be classified as a transsexual.[57]

CHAPTER THREE
EXISTING THEORIES OF HOMOSEXUALITY

In general, theories are explanations of why we behave as we do.[1] Theories give us clues about possible causes of behavior.[2] If causes can be identified then intervention and remediation can occur. For example, there is a theoretical hypothesis (with strong empirical support) that a person who was abused as a child has an increased risk of being a child abuser.[3] This proposition states that *one* cause of being an adult abuser is prior victimization. Knowing this, a parent can reduce the chances of a child growing up to be abusive (and violent) if the parent guides the child with warmth, support, and firm but loving discipline.[4]

This solution, of discovering and then controlling causes of behavior, is not as simple as it appears because most complex social behaviors (such as those associated with abuse or homosexuality) are influenced by multiple factors acting over many years. Identifying and controlling one or two causes that may contribute to the undesirable behavior may not be enough to prevent the occurrence of that unwanted behavior. In the case of homosexuality, there may be many causes and several competing theories that attempt to explain homosexual behavior.

Some argue that homosexuality must be genetic—a person is born that way.[5] A few assert that homosexuality is a result of too little or too much testosterone (the male sex hormone that is responsible for masculine characteristics) in the body during prenatal or postnatal development.[6] Others indicate that a cold, rejecting father is a root cause.[7] A few suggest that sexual molestation and early sexual promiscuity may promote homosexual behavior.[8] All of these explanations, both biological and environmental, have some empirical support but remain controversial.[9]

Biogenic Theories

Biogenic refers to the effects of genes and hormones on human behavior.[10] These theories suggest that homosexual behavior is mostly due to structural differences in the brain,[11] prenatal or postnatal exposure to sex hormones,[12] or variations in chromosomes that may influence sexual behavior.[13] All these biological theories assert that there is some innate cause for homosexuality.[14]

Byne, a physician and biologist, explained that there are direct and indirect biogenic models of homosexuality. A direct model stipulates that "genes and hormones exert their influence on sexual orientation by directly organizing the neural circuits that mediate sexual orientation."[15] In other words, biology may hard-wire the brain for homosexual attraction, fantasy, and behavior. An indirect pathway suggests that biology influences temperament (or other personality traits) that in turn "influence the formative experiences that contribute to the social acquisition of sexual orientation."[16] For example, a child could be genetically predisposed to be shy, sensitive, artistic, and non-athletic and then various experiences over the years work in favor of a homosexual outcome.

Is There A Gay Gene?

The argument is made by many homosexuals and pro-gay scientists that there is a gene that determines sexual orientation. In order to judge the merits of this position one should understand basic biological facts.

Inside each body cell are 46 chromosomes, 23 inherited from the mother and 23 from the father. Chromosomes are squiggly little strings of DNA (**D**eoxyribo**N**ucleic **A**cid). Microscopically each chromosome looks something like a tightly twister ladder with rungs in the middle supported by side bars.[17] The rungs of the ladder are composed of "nucleotides" or "nitrogenous bases". There are four nucleotides: thymine linked to adenine (T-A links) or its reverse (A-T), and cytosine and guanine (C-G links) or its reverse (G-C). These nucleotides (the rungs of the ladder) are connected by sugar-phosphate molecules which act like the side bars of the ladder to give structural support to the DNA.[18]

A gene is a short segment of DNA in a particular location on a specific chromosome.[19] An average length of about 1500 nucleotides makes a gene. Geneticists believe there are 20-25,000 genes in human DNA.[20] Genes carry instructions (like a building construction blue-print) to manufacture proteins or to activate or de-activate other genes.[21] Single genes usually make one protein or part of one protein.

The word protein comes from the Greek "proteos" meaning 'of primary importance.' A protein is a long chain of amino acids folded up into a specific three dimensional shape. There are 20 common amino acids but these can combine in various ways to make thousands of proteins. Proteins made in cells may remain in the cell to support cell structure and function or may be excreted and exported to other parts of the body. Examples of proteins include enzymes, antibodies, and some hormones and neurotransmitters.

Now, knowing what a gene is and what a gene does, one can ask the question, "Is there a gay gene?" Given conventional wisdom, the answer may surprise the reader. There is a clear consensus among scientists that a gay gene *does not* exist. Complex psycho-social behaviors such as sexual orientation cannot be directly traced to the activity of a single gene or even a group of genes.[22]

Here are some examples of what scientists say about the gay gene theory. Dr. Francis S. Collins (MD and PhD), head of The Human Genome Project, concluded:

> There is an inescapable component of heritability to many human behavioral traits. For virtually none of them is heredity ever close to predictive ... An area of particularly strong public interest is the genetic basis of homosexuality. Evidence [indicates] that sexual orientation is genetically influenced but not hardwired by DNA, and that whatever genes are involved represent predispositions, not predeterminations.[23]

Biologist Richard Lewontin and colleagues stated:

> Up to the present time no one has ever been able to relate any aspect of human social behavior to any particular gene or set of genes, and no one has ever suggested an experimental plan for doing so. Thus, all statements about the genetic basis of human social traits are necessarily purely speculative, no matter how positive they seem to be.[24]

Edward Stein a pro-gay psychologist explains:

> Genes in themselves cannot directly specify any behavior or psychological phenomenon. Instead, genes direct a particular pattern of RNA synthesis, which in turn may influence the development of psychological dispositions and the expression of behaviors. There are many intervening pathways between a gene and a disposition or a behavior, and even more intervening variables between a gene and a pattern that involves both thinking and behaviors...No one has presented evidence in support of such a simple and direct link between genes and sexual orientation.[25]

Catherine Baker, a behavioral psychologist, concurs:

> Many people think that a gene controls a behavioral trait. This is genetic determinism, the belief that the development of an organism is determined solely by genetic factors. Genetic determinism is a false belief. It comes from misunderstandings of scientific research... The fact is that so far, scientific research has not confirmed any one-to-one correspondence between a gene and a [complex] human behavior. Behavior results from the activity of multiple genes amidst the influence of multiple environmental factors.[26]

Many misinformed people believe that a single gene determines a specific behavior. For example some assume there is an alcoholic gene, a manic-depression gene, or a gay gene. However, "It is an oversimplification to say that any gene is 'the gene for a trait.' Each gene simply specifies one of the proteins involved in the process [of gene-environment interaction]."[27] Except for a few rare physical abnormalities such as Huntington's disease, cystic fibrosis, PKU, and achondroplasia, there is no evidence of a direct causative link between a single gene and complex psychosocial behavior such as sexual preference.[28]

Robert Plomin a well-regarded geneticist concludes that "genes do not act as master puppeteers within us. They are chemical structures that control the production of proteins; thereby indirectly affecting behavior ... Genes do not determine one's destiny."[29] Plomin provides a useful analogy about how genes and the environment interact to produce behavior.

A sailboat needs both sails [environment] and a hull [genes]. The 'behavior' of a sailboat (speed, turning ability, and direction) depends on the design of its sails and the design of its hull. The aerodynamic shape of the sails, their number and size, and their positioning are important. The depth, width, length, and shape of the hull are also important. Obviously, for sailboats, there can be no behavior without both sails and hull, but this does not restrict us from asking about the independent contributions of sail design and hull design to the behavior of sailboats…Behavior requires both genes and environment.[30]

Yet, even this example is flawed. The missing factor in Plomin's analogy is the captain at the helm of the ship. That captain is moral agency which we discuss in detail in Chapter 4. Regardless of sails (environmental factors) and hull design (genetic predispositions), the captain can make moral decisions independent of both sails and hull. The skipper may be constrained by forces beyond his control, but he is not absolutely determined by them. The British poet William Ernest Henley (1849–1903) communicates this idea in his famous poem "Invictus" (Latin for unconquerable): "It matters not how strait the gate, how charged with punishment the scroll. I am the master of my fate: I am the captain of my soul." The poet sees what scientists fail to recognize: Agency intervenes in the interplay between genes and environment.

Consider the recent example of Michael Glatze, founder of *Young Gay American Magazine*, film producer, pro-gay lecturer and author, and well-recognized leader in the gay movement. At age 14 he believed himself to be gay, but at age 30 he "seriously began to doubt" what he was doing.[31] He explained:

> Knowing no one who I could approach with my questions and my doubts, I turned to God … It became clear to me that homosexuality prevents us from finding our true selves … I was leading a movement of sin and corruption … Now I know that homosexuality is lust and pornography wrapped into one. I'll never let anybody try to convince me otherwise… Healing from the wounds caused by homosexuality is not easy—there's little support. In my experience, coming out from under the influence of the homosexual mindset was the most liberating, beautiful and astonishing thing I've ever experienced … I believe that

all people, intrinsically know the truth. I believe that is why Christianity scares people so much. It reminds them of their conscience, which we all possess. Conscience tell us right from wrong and is a guide by which we can grow and become stronger and freer human beings.[32]

Do Abnormal Levels of Sex Hormones Account for Homosexuality?

The hormone theory is the second biological explanation of homosexuality.[33] Hormones (from the Greek, "to spur on") are powerful chemicals produced by endocrine glands (e.g., hypothalamus, pituitary, thyroid, ovaries, and testes) that circulate freely in the bloodstream and affect a wide range of cell structures and functioning.[34] The "prenatal hormone hypothesis" suggests that if a fetus is exposed to too much or too little sex hormones during prenatal (or even perinatal) development, this will affect not only the internal and external genitalia but also the brain, which may in turn, influence gender identity and sexual orientation.[35] The theory suggests that a female fetus exposed to too much endogenous or exogenous androgens will have a higher chance of becoming lesbian; and a male fetus under exposed to androgens will more likely self-report as gay than those with normal hormones levels.[36]

This hypothesis is impossible to test directly because hormone experimentation with humans is illegal and unethical. Researchers can only take advantage of "natural experiments" in which pregnant women were inadvertently exposed to sex hormones or children who are born with endocrine disorders such as congenital adrenal hyperplasia or androgen insensitivity syndrome.[37] Various studies that have attempted to test the prenatal hormone hypothesis have proven inconclusive.[38] Two doctors concluded that "studies of testosterone levels [the male sex hormone] have not shown a deficiency in male homosexuals or an excess in lesbians."[39] They conclude that "the data do not support a causal connection between hormones and human sexual orientation."[40]

Others disagree and interpret existing research as supportive of the prenatal hormone theory.[41] Supporters look to animal research where there is evidence with mice that androgen treatment of female fetuses in utero will produce male-type sex behavior in females and removal of normal fetal androgen secretion in male fetuses produces female type behavior.[42] Yet, as endocrinologist Louis Gooren concluded, "The mechanism of sexual differentiation in laboratory animals is clearly orchestrated by gonadal steroids", but "in humans the mechanism of brain sexual dimorphism [is] not yet certain... [and] we are far away from any comprehensive understanding of hormonal imprinting on gender identity formation.[43]

Overall, there is no clear and convincing evidence that homosexuality results from abnormal levels of hormones in humans.[44] Bancroft has stated that genes or hormones may influence sexual orientation, but their influences "need to be understood as interacting with the effects of social and cognitive learning rather than having direct effects of their own."[45] We concur.

Another Challenge to Biogenic Explanations of Homosexuality

Many researchers and gay activists over the past three decades have reported that children of gays or lesbians are no more likely to be homosexual than a child from a heterosexual family.[46] But in most cases, the children of these homosexual couples are biologically related to one of the gay or lesbian partners.[47] If genes determined homosexual behavior, then the children of gays and lesbians should show higher rates of homosexuality than children reared in heterosexual homes. If they don't, then genes can't cause homosexuality.[48] Yet, gays and gay activists continue to claim that children raised by homosexuals are no more likely to become gay or lesbian than children reared by two heterosexual parents.

A few studies, however, suggest that children of gay and lesbian parents are more likely to become homosexual than children reared in heterosexual families.[49] Nevertheless, these studies cannot prove a biological basis for homosexuality. The psychosocial environment in the gay parents' home could account for their children's increased propensity for homosexual behavior. Gay parents model homosexual behavior. They teach their children that homosexuality is healthy and normal, and they socialize with other gays and lesbians. All of these environmental influences could increase the likelihood for a same-sex preference.

Conclusions Regarding the Biological Explanations of Homosexuality

Byne and Parsons reviewed 135 research and essay articles on the biological evidence for homosexuality and concluded, "There is no evidence at present to substantiate a biologic theory, just as there is no evidence to support any singular psychosocial explanation" of homosexuality.[50] Even gay advocates such as Szuchman and colleagues concluded that the scientific evidence for a biological cause of homosexual behavior is "remarkably flawed, such that no unbiased view for or against many of these factors [i.e., biogenetic causes] is possible ... We still have no good evidence of biological influences on sexual preference or sexual orientation."[51] Gay advocates Parker and DeCecco conceded that "research into possible biological bases of sexual preference has failed to produce any conclusive evidence."[52]

Friedman and Downey noted that credible evidence for a simple biological explanation of homosexuality is lacking, concluding that "human sexual orientation is complex and diversely experienced and that a biological-psycho-social model best fits the current state of knowledge in the field."[53] More recently, they have taken an even stronger position: "At clinical conferences one often hears ... that homosexual orientation is fixed and unmodifiable. Neither assertion is true ... The assertion that homosexuality is genetic is so reductionistic that it must be dismissed out of hand as a general principle of psychology."[54]

In addition, the activist researchers Drs. Anne Fausto-Sterling and Camille Paglia (both self-identified lesbians) are even more insistent that homosexuality is not simply a matter of biology. Fausto-Sterling who is a developmental biologist, referring to the biological argument, concludes, "It provides a legal argument that is, at this moment, actually having some sway in court. For me, it is a very shaky place. It's bad science and bad politics. It seems to me that the way we consider homosexuality in our culture is an ethical and a moral question."[55] Dr. Paglia concludes, "No one is born gay. The idea is ridiculous ... homosexuality is an adaptation, not an inborn trait."[56] Elliot Valenstein summarizes:

> Most recent claims that a gene has been discovered that causes alcoholism, schizophrenia, [or] homosexuality ... have proven illusory ... Genes do not produce behavioral or mental states. Genes carry the instructions and template for producing and assembling amino acids and proteins into anatomical

structures. Behavior and mental traits, however, are the product of an interaction between anatomical structure and experience ... Even where there is compelling evidence that some behavioral or mental trait is influenced by genetic factors it is almost always a predisposition, not a certainty ... A predisposition is not a cause.[57]

We recognize that genes may have an indirect influence on homosexuality by their effects on personality, temperament, and physical activity. But we believe that genes and hormones are neither a necessary nor a sufficient cause of homosexual behavior.

Environmental Theories

Environmental theories suggest that homosexual behavior is a result of socialization, learning, and conditioning. Two theories will be reviewed: the psychoanalytic explanation and the social learning theory.

Psychoanalytic Theory

This theory was developed by psychoanalytic therapists over a period of many years, beginning with Sigmund Freud.[58] In essence, a man's or a woman's homosexual behavior is rooted in pathological parent-child relationships. In most cases the child is exposed to a father who is weak, uninvolved, rejecting and/or abusive.[59] The child's mother is often dominant, overprotective, smothering, and/or seductive.[60] The child's intimate and continual interaction with these parents produces a Gender Identity deficit, and the child fails to internalize a strong sense of manhood or womanhood.[61] Davies and Rentzer commented on this process: "Many people experience some degree of rejection in their early years. But when a little boy fails to connect with his dad and a little girl doesn't form a close relationship with her mother, the groundwork is laid for future gender identity struggles."[62]

To illustrate the psychoanalytic explanation of homosexuality, Zucker and Bradley report on their clinical work with a four year old boy named Timmy.[63] The parents were concerned with their son's expressed desire to be girl, his preference for girl playmates and female role playing, his pervasive cross-dressing, and his avoidance of rough-and-tumble games. Analysis of their family dynamics revealed a dominant mother with an intense, overly close emotional relationship to her son. The father was weak and uninvolved. Both parents admitted they had been "positive and encouraging" of Timmy's cross-gender behavior and would "fuss over" him when he "paraded around in his dresses."[64] This example reveals the classic family characteristics associated with a homosexual outcome, including the smothering mother, the pathetic father, and both parents' encouragement of the child's cross-gender behavior.

In an earlier study, Wolff found that some lesbians in her sample came from families with absent or abusive fathers and mothers who were cold and rejecting. For women, sexual abuse engendered a fear and loathing of men, and they tended to retreat to the safety and security of women.[65] Loney, using a sample of 11 lesbians and 12 heterosexual women, found that the lesbians reported higher levels of parent-child conflict and marital conflict between their parents. The lesbians also had fathers who were "neglecting, moody and mean" and mothers who were "weak, self-absorbed and fearful."[66] Loney surmised that the girls' homosexual orientation was a "compromise solution" for failure to comfortably identify with their mothers and an "unsatisfactory relationship with their fathers."[67]

Zucker and Bradley studied 26 girls with Gender Identity disorder (a predictor of later homosexuality) and found several commonalities. Thirty-eight percent of the mothers of these girls had severe psychiatric problems, 77% of the mothers suffered from chronic depression. Thirty percent of the mothers reported "severe and chronic sexual abuse of an incestuous nature" and communicated a message to their daughter "that being female was unsafe."[68] Many of the mothers "regarded the female gender role with disdain."[69] "The mothers had a great deal of difficulty in instilling in their daughters a sense of pride and confidence about being female."[70] The girls perceived their mothers "as weak, incompetent, or helpless."[71] Fifty percent of the girls reported "severe" abuse at the hands of their fathers or brothers. Though the clinical evidence is not as clear for lesbians as it is for gay men, it appears that unhealthy family relationships and sexual abuse may increase a girl's susceptibility to engaging in homosexual behavior.[72]

In sum, psychoanalytic theorists suggest that the main cause of homosexuality is disordered parent-child relationships where the child is treated with little love and support by the same-sex parent, or with outright disdain, rejection, or abuse. This can elicit early feelings of "being different" at a young age, or as some gay men report, "I've always felt this attraction to men." These early feelings, however, are not evidence of genetic determinism, but of the subconscious recognition at a young age of the disordered parent-child relationship and the longing for an appropriate emotional bonding to someone of the same sex. The child unconsciously rejects identification with the same-sex parent and turns to same-sex peers or adults for love, support, and affirmation. These relationships can then become eroticized.

Social Learning Theory

Social Learning Theory explains how we learn complex behaviors primarily through observation and modeling of the actions, emotions, and attitudes of significant others.[73] Significant others are persons we value or hold in high regard—persons who have the power to reward or punish us. Essentially, this theory suggests that adolescents learn sexual behavior and sexual preference from parents, peers, and the media (e.g., TV, movies, the internet, and music). Then youth are rewarded or punished for their sexual attitudes and behaviors.[74]

For example, suppose a young teen has tried to flirt with girls only to be routinely rebuffed—this punishment would decrease his efforts to approach girls in the future. He finds some gratification (a reward) viewing online pornography. Furthermore, he retreats to the company of other boys who have little interest in girls. In such company, he finds support and friendship, and feels the first inklings of homosexuality.

Another source of learning about same-sex behavior is through the media which includes TV, movies, music, magazines.[75] In general, American children are being sexualized early in development. The onslaught of sexual messages, both heterosexual and homosexual, engulfs our youth in a culture of promiscuity.[76] A recent Kaiser Family Foundation study, entitled *Sex on TV*, indicated that the percentage of TV shows with sexual content has increased from 56% in 1998 to 70% in 2005. There are nearly seven sex-related scenes per hour in prime-time TV programs targeted at teens.[77] Among the top teen shows, only 10% include any references to the risks or responsibilities of non-marital sex. The dominant message of the media is that youth should become sexually active and experiment with sexual behavior, even with homosexual behavior.[78]

Two studies by the Rand Corporation demonstrated that "watching TV shows with sexual content hastens the initiation of teen sexual activity."[79] Non-marital sex is glamorized by the media, and homosexuality and bisexuality are considered "cool" or "hip."[80] The media is overwhelmingly gay affirming.[81] Hence, some youth may be tempted to try out the thinking and behavior of homosexuality because of the positive role modeling of homosexuality in the media.

Social learning theory can also account for the role of serious emotional trauma, such as sexual abuse, in the etiology of homosexual behavior.[82] Many adult homosexuals have reported childhood sexual abuse, often by a homosexual adult, in greater proportion than that found in heterosexual comparison groups.[83] For example, in one study of over 1000 adult homosexual and bisexual men, 37% reported they had been encouraged or forced (between the ages of 9 and 12) to have sex with older men.[84] Bradford, Ryan, and Rothblum found that 25% of about 2000 lesbian women had been sexually abused or raped as children.[85]

Simari and Baskin interviewed 54 gay men and 29 lesbians. Nearly half (46%) of the men and 36% of the women had experienced homosexual incest.[86] Yet, in various national, random samples of the general population, only about 17% of women and 5% of men reported incidents of sexual abuse during childhood.[87] Holmes and Slap found that "abused adolescents, particularly those victimized by males, were up to seven times more likely to self-identify as gay or bisexual than peers who had not been abused."[88]

Rekers reported the case of Shawn, who never thought about homosexual activity until he was thirteen years old and in a foster home where he shared a bedroom with the sixteen year old son of the foster parents. The sixteen-year-old forced Shawn into oral-genital activities at night, threatening to beat him up if he told the parents. At first, Shawn felt disgusted and angry, but he developed a preference for homosexual activity over time. Rekers found that "seduction by an older person of the same sex" was a common occurrence in the lives of homosexual men.[89]

Roesler and Deishner interviewed 60 non-clinical (not in therapy) homosexuals and found that in almost all cases the men stated that they had same-sex experiences prior to labeling themselves as homosexuals.[90] Shrier and Johnson reported that in a clinical sample of 40 homosexuals, and in a matched sample of 40 heterosexual teenagers, 58% of the homosexual adolescents had been sexually molested by a homosexual adult prior to puberty, while only 8% of the heterosexual boys reported sexual abuse. One half of the teens engaged in same-sex behavior "linked their homosexuality to their sexual victimization experience."[91]

Consider the following excerpt from the Greg Louganis Story. He was an Olympic gold medal diver. In his book he revealed his history of sexual abuse, which included the following excerpt:

> He [a man the same age as Greg's father], put his arms around me and kissed me. I really liked being held, and I was thrilled that his guy found me attractive...I thought over time that I'd feel less ashamed about what I was doing, but it only got worse. The age difference bothered me more, and he couldn't exactly be a part of my life. I felt stupid telling him what I was doing at school, and I couldn't introduce him to any of my class-mates. I hated the separation and secrecy, but I kept going back for the affection, the holding, the cuddling---more than the sex. I was starved for affection, and he was happy to give it to me...it upset me that he was so much older, not because I felt molested or anything---I had been more than a willing partner, but the difference in our ages somehow made the experience even more shameful...At some point he told me he was concerned about seeing me because I was under eighteen. Apparently, he'd been jailed in the past for picking up minors.[92]

In a recent study, Tomeo and colleagues surveyed 942 adults (mostly non-clinical college students from Central California). Forty-six percent of the homosexual men and 22% of the lesbian women had been molested by a same-sex adult at the average age of 13. Only 7% of the heterosexual men and 1% of the heterosexual women had been molested by a same-sex adult. What is even more revealing is that "68% of the gay males in this study and 38% of the lesbian females ... did not identify as homosexual until af-ter the molestation."[93] Thus, the trauma of sexual molestation may, in some unknown way, confuse the child's sexual preference and trigger homoerotic feelings and behavior.

These studies taken together suggest that childhood sexual abuse may be a contributing factor to later homosexual behavior. It should be remem-bered, however, that connection (or correlation) may not mean causation, and many homosexuals do not report a history of sexual abuse. It should be noted that some men who have been sexually abused often have difficul-ties in viewing the experience as abusive because "allowing" such abuse is incompatible with masculinity. Thus, "sexual abuse" may not be reported by some homosexual men.

In summary, Social Learning Theory suggests that there may be some environmental influences on the development of homosexual behavior. Parents, peers, the media, and traumatic events such as sexual molestation, could contribute to a homosexual outcome. There are, however, many social scientists that reject any and all environmental explanations for homosexuality.[94] Gay psychiatrist Richard Isay claims there is no evidence that homosexuality is due to childhood sexual abuse. Isay adds that "very, very few mental health professionals hold on to the notion that environment molds sexual orientation."[95] His conclusion, however, is not accurate. And here is just one example.

In 1995, Drs. Vreeland and Gallagher surveyed over five hundred psychiatrists across the nation asking their opinions about the causes or origins of male homosexuality.[96] The doctors were asked to rate the causes of homosexuality using a 5-point scale. The number 1 represented a factor that had "*no relationship to homosexuality*" (i.e., it was not a cause of homosexuality), 2 represented a factor that was "*weakly related*" to homosexuality, 3 represented "*somewhat related*", 4 meant "*strongly related*", and 5 meant "*very strongly related.*" If a factor was rated **4** or **5**, then it was a probable cause of homosexual behavior. Their rankings are listed here:

1. Genetic Inheritance	3.0
2. Prenatal hormones	2.8
3. Hypothalamus differences	2.7
4. Brain organization	2.6
5. Dominant mother	2.2
6. Weak, cold father	2.1
7. Seduction by same sex adult	2.1
8. Cross dressing by the child	2.1
9. Parents wish for opposite sex child	1.9
10. Parents dysfunctional marriage	1.9

Biogenetic factors (e.g., genes or hormones) were the higher ranked factors, but the values of the biogenic factors—between 3.0 and 2.6—only indicated that the factors were "*somewhat related*" to male homosexuality—not "*4.0 strongly related*" and "*5.0 very strongly related*". Environmental factors (e.g., a dominant mother, a weak father, seduction by a same sex adult, parent's dysfunctional marriage) with an average mean of 2.0 were also identified as possible contributors to a homosexual outcome.

Interactional Theory

Daryl Bem's interactional theory combines the indirect effects of genetics with environmental influences to explain homosexuality. Bem posits that genes or hormones do not directly cause sexual preference but do influence a child's temperament and activity level, which in turn influences the child's preferred friends, activities, and emotional responses.[97] For example, "Boys who are not particularly active or aggressive, and girls who are more aggressive than their peers, develop gender-nonconforming play patterns and have more opposite-sex playmates."[98] Such children may be rejected by same-sex peers and so they turn to opposite-sex peers for companionship. Over time a youth may develop an erotic attraction to same-sex peers because they are seen as having "different traits. In essence, these youth sexualize traits which they view as lacking in themselves.

Stein also takes an interactional perspective and suggests that there may be some biological predisposition for homosexuality, but that predisposition must interact with environmental factors to eventually produce a homosexual outcome. He calls his theory *non-determinism*. "Non-determinism is the view that a person does not consciously choose his or her sexual orientation, but that indirect choices [influenced by biological factors] play a role in the development of sexual orientation."[99] In other words, early in life a child may make small choices that may unintentionally affect the child's later sexual desires and preferences.

For example, suppose a little boy, born with a gentle, sensitive temperament—whose mother would have preferred a girl—was encouraged by his parents to prefer girl's clothes, toys, and tea parties. Because of his innate personality and support from his mother, he may be persuaded to play with dolls instead of throwing balls. As he grows he is kept away from rough-and-tumble play (or he chooses to avoid it) and is exposed to music and poetry where he has some talent. These conditions may later indirectly influence his emerging sexual orientation.[100] As a teenage boy he may attempt to flirt with girls, but due to his appearance or mannerisms, he is rejected. In addition, his father may ridicule him for his "sissy-like behavior." The cumulative effect of innate temperament and social conditioning may increase the likelihood that the youth will consider homosexuality as an option.

In sum, Interactional Theory seems to be a reasonable alternative to either the biogenic or social learning explanations. Interactional theory combines elements of both and proposes that biologically based personality traits nurtured in a particular family and social environment may lead to homosexuality.

A Final Comment about Theories of Homosexuality

The search for a "cause" for homosexuality is important for social and political reasons. If homosexuality was shown to have strong biological roots, then opposition to it would diminish.[101] Medinger suggests that gay activ- ists are "determined to find proof that homosexuality is hard-wired into the child ... then a just society will surely have to recognize homosexuality as an acceptable way of life."[102] LeVay, a self-identified gay and former scientist at the Salk Institute in San Francisco, concurred, "People who think that gays and lesbians are born that way are more likely to support gay rights."[103]

In this debate about the etiology of homosexuality it is important to distinguish between two concepts: a *cause* versus a *contributing factor*. In common usage the word *cause* denotes an exact, specific, and straight-for-ward reason for the occurrence of a phenomenon. For example, the cause of my cold is a virus. The cause of my flushed face is embarrassment because I forgot my lines in the community play. A contributing factor, however, is not a direct, unambiguous cause—but only a condition that, in combina-tion with other conditions, may increase the likelihood of a certain out-come. A contributing factor does not absolutely *cause* a thing to happen. A contributing factor is like finding extra change in your pocket. The fact that you have the coins does not force you to spend them on something. Having the unexpected money only increases the chance that you might purchase something. What you do with the money is still up to you.

In medicine and engineering, causes are often easily identified, and effective cures for disease or construction methods for building a bridge, are easily implemented. But in the study of human social behavior, causes are difficult to find and to prove absolutely. At best, social scientists usu-ally identify a list of contributing factors. Such is the case with homo-sexuality. At this time, direct causes have not been found. Yet, contrib-uting factors have been identified such as poor parent-child relationships and sexual abuse. There is one thing that has not been recognized in any of the previous theories about the causes of homosexuality and that is moral agency, or the ability to make choices about one's sexual behavior. Agency is the topic of the next chapter.

CHAPTER FOUR
AGENCY IN SEXUAL BEHAVIOR

Many social scientists believe that an interactional model—combining biological, family, and social influences—makes the most sense as an explanation for homosexuality. However, this model possesses one major drawback: it fails to consider moral agency and choice in shaping homosexual behavior.

Biological theories suggest that a force of nature (genes or prenatal hormones) causes homosexuality, and environmental theories posit that social experiences (e.g., unhealthy parent-child interaction and/or sexual abuse) push the individual into homosexual behavior. But little is said by either theoretical camp about the person's own active participation in development of sexual preference.

"Conspicuously absent from most theorizing on the origins of sexual orientation is an active role of the individual in constructing his or her own [sexual] identity,"[1] say Byne and Parsons, following their comprehensive review of studies on homosexuality. Diamond also notes that while biology may bias the person's sexual orientation, individual behavior remains flexible when responding to environmental influences, and free choice must also be considered.[2]

We are not saying that homosexual attraction is consciously chosen. Sexual feelings are not necessarily selected, but may come unbidden at certain times during development because of situational factors and prior personal experiences. But we are saying that homoerotic feelings can be fostered or strengthened by small and simple choices people make, and that eventually a moral choice is made to engage in homosexual behavior.

It is generally believed that humans are free to make behavioral choices, regardless of past experiences or current conditions. This concept of "agency" implies choice, free will, or self-determination which is the ability to make decisions independent of past choices or circumstances. Some theorists argue that present and future choices can be limited or restricted, but they are not absolutely determined by past choices and experiences.[3] Humans make conscious choices and are able, in most situations, to alter their thinking, emotions, and behaviors.[4]

Intentional action is no doubt a driving force in our human natures. Consider the experience of Viktor Frankl, a psychologist and survivor of a Nazi concentration camp:

> But what about human liberty? Is there no spiritual freedom in regard to behavior and reaction to any given surroundings? Is that theory true which would have us believe that man is no more than a product of many conditional and environmental factors—be they of a biological, psychological or sociological nature?... Does man have no choice of action? ...The experiences of [Nazi prison] camp life show that man does have a choice of action...There were always choices to make. Every day, every hour offered the opportunity to make a decision... In the final analysis it becomes clear that the sort of person the prisoner became was the result of an inner decision and not the result of camp influences alone. Fundamentally, therefore, any man can, even under such circumstances, decide what shall become of him—mentally and spiritually.[5]

In a similar way, a particular individual may have been predisposed to homosexuality due to biology, family pathology, sexual abuse, or the enticements of peers and the media. But there is still an element of choice involved. In other words, in addition to biology and environmental influences, a person over a period of months or years can make decisions that lead to the eventual involvement in homosexual behavior. Lesbian activist Camille Paglia makes the point well. She notes that there is choice in all conscious behavior, sexual or otherwise.[6]

Present theories do not recognize the individual's active assent and purposeful participation in choosing sexual behavior or creating a sexual identity. Glock, a sociologist at UC Berkeley, explained that,

> Scientists, in their search for explanations, effectively ignore free will as a possible causal agent. This is not because scientists do not believe in the existence of free will. At a philosophical level, we suspect that most count themselves as believers. Certainly, in their everyday lives, they think and act as if free will exists. When they function as scientists, however, they have not found a means to establish if free will may be operative as a determinate of human behavior.[7]

Glock points out that while science gives no credence to free will as a possible contributor to behavior, science offers no proof of its non-existence, either. Many social scientists refuse to acknowledge free will in their research and theories, yet they believe *themselves* to be in possession of it![8] However, many psychologists and psychiatrists refuse to consider that agency has anything to do with homosexual behavior.

A Religious Understanding of Moral Agency

Williams proposed a view of agency that is a two-fold process: first, there must be "knowledge of truth," and second, one can make the decision to "live truthfully" or not. Agency does not consist chiefly in "doing what we want" (i.e., choosing between amoral alternatives), but in "doing what we should do" (i.e., knowing true principles and deciding to live by them).[9] "Human freedom does not simply mean doing whatever one wants," Needleman explains. "That is a childish idea. A mature vision of freedom— a religious vision of freedom—implies voluntary obedience to the higher law of conscience [i.e., the laws of God]."[10]

It is our belief that agency can only exist within a universe where some things are right and good (for individuals and society) and other things are wrong, hurtful, and destructive. A moral universe can only be created and structured by a divine creator, because every man-made form of morality will eventually breakdown into individual preferences and relativistic choices. Like Novak, we believe that there is no agency without morality:

> In the absence of judgment [i.e., a moral standard], freedom [i.e., agency] cannot thrive. If nothing matters, freedom is

pointless. If one choice is as good as another, choice is merely a preference. Without standards, no one is free, but only a slave to impulses coming from who knows where.[11]

Freedom without the guidance of moral principle is not freedom, Needleman explains, but simply devolves into self-interest and personal gain.[12] Thus, agency cannot exist in a moral vacuum.

Psychologist Allen Bergin explains, "For sexual expression to nurture relationships and produce joy, it must be guided by spiritual principles. Behavior outside these principles puts at risk our ability to ultimately attain the highest joys of sexual expression."[13] Such principles come from God and exist "independently of anyone's construction of them," says Fischer.[14] Moral agency is the ability to understand the reality of our heterosexual natures, and the conscious, deliberate choice to live as heterosexual beings.

Another way to understand the role of moral agency in same-sex behavior is to consider the words of Paul, the Christian missionary who lived during the time of Jesus. He traveled and preached extensively from Palestine to Greece from AD 50 to AD 65. In Paul's second epistle to the believers in Corinth, Greece (circa AD 57), he made a surprising revelation: "There was given me a thorn in the flesh, the messenger of Satan to buffet me" (New Testament, II Corinthians 12: 7). We think Paul was saying this:

> I could become arrogant and proud because of all my accomplishments. I might even believe I can save myself by my good works and many years of service to God. But God has given me a weakness that humbles me, and reminds me of my dependence on Him and that it is by His grace that I am saved.

Paul's "thorn" was probably some immoral feeling or sinful inclination that he struggled with for many years. Three times Paul tried to pray it away and asked God to remove the unholy thing. But God declined and said, "My grace is sufficient for thee, and your weakness will make you stronger in the end because you will rely on me, the Lord" (II Corinthians 12:9). Note that Paul's thorn was not something he acted upon. It was something he felt, and felt strongly, but apparently did not do.

The scriptures never mention Paul's wife or family, so let's suppose he struggled with homosexual attraction. That was the thorn in his side. We have no idea what it really was, but it works for the sake of illustrating a point.

We, like Paul, have "weaknesses of the flesh." We experience immoral, illegal, unethical, and unhealthy inclinations from time to time. These proclivities can include over indulgence in eating, drinking, spending money, and various desires to lie, to steal, to inflict harm, or to have lustful, covetous, or vengeful thoughts. Like Paul, we try hard not to do any of these things. Of course at times we fail, but more often than not we succeed in keeping these baser inclinations far from fruition. We are able to do that because we possess moral agency. Moral agency is the ability to choose right over wrong, good over evil, kindness instead of cruelty. With agency one can choose not to act upon an unethical or immoral impulse.

But one could ask, "Why do we even have these feelings in the first place?" We have an answer, and it might explain some cases of homosexuality where biological and environmental contributors seem to be lacking or are not readily apparent. From a Christian perspective, the primary purpose of life is a test of will. Will we follow God's laws and keep his commandments, or will we rebel and choose evil. Evil is any action in opposition to God's will and divine laws. Evil behavior is innately self-destructive and harmful to others. Opposition—a choice between good and evil—is part of God's plan in almost all aspects of life; otherwise agency could not exist.

If we are free to choose, there must be choices. One of the most important choices for a Christian (or Jew, or Muslim, or Hindu) is to marry, have children, and find joy, peace, and contentment in a long-term, monogamous marriage. In opposition to this plan is the path of sexual immorality which includes fornication, adultery, incest and homosexuality.

In some cases of homosexuality there may be no antecedents that triggered homoerotic feelings. There may have been no adverse life events that misdirected the normal heterosexual trajectory. Sometimes there may be no identifiable cause. Incompetent parents, poverty, or abuse are not to blame; neither are promiscuous peers, or the influence of immoral media or pornography. It may seem that the person's homoerotic feelings emerged on their own without conscious volition or deliberate action by the individual.

Given our interpretation of moral agency, homosexual attraction for many individuals may simply be a test—a thorn in the flesh—a specific trial that some must endure while most others do not. This challenge is not unlike others who are tested with a severe disability, a life of poverty, or with over-eating, or addictions to alcohol, gambling, or pornography.

But whatever the test, God has promised a way out. Paul gives us hope: "*There is no temptation you will experience that is not common to humanity;*

but God will not suffer you to be tempted above what you are able to bear; but with temptation He will make a way to escape" (I Cor. 10:13). This indicates that one's moral agency is never usurped by feelings or inclinations. Homosexual desires may be strong and persistent, but they are never so strong as to deprive the person of the freedom to choose moral conduct.[15]

Agency Can Be Compromised

Agency, the opportunity to live by true principles is easier for some than for others. A person without the light and knowledge of true principles, or who was reared in a corrupt and depraved family, or who is subjected to a social environment of promiscuity and violence, or who has made immoral choices in the past, may find it more difficult to exercise agency and choose right behavior.[16] For example, compare homosexuality to an addiction like alcohol or gambling. A person may have an innate susceptibility to alcohol or personality traits that put him at risk for gambling, but in the beginning the whiskey or the poker games were choices. Over time, the booze or blackjack became a compulsion, and eventually an addiction which makes the exercise of agency more difficult.

Homosexual behavior may develop in a similar way. The first homosexual experience is chosen and intentional—though made more likely to occur by prior environmental conditions, or emotional or biological predispositions. But the more one engages in homosexual behavior, the more the behaviors become habitual and compulsive.[17] Neural pathways in the brain are strengthened by repetition of the behavior, and emotional-social responses are conditioned through integration into a homosexual lifestyle. In small ways the brain and body chemistry are eventually changed to reinforce the homosexual behavior.

Over time, the person has diminished ability to reduce or stop the homosexual behavior. If asked, a man (or woman) trapped in alcohol or gambling will respond that "No, I didn't choose this! Why would anyone choose this life?" He assumes he never "chose" because he doesn't recall making a conscious decision to be a drunk or a gambler. Likewise, a gay man or a lesbian may not recall "choosing" to be homosexual, but forgetfulness does not eliminate the possibility that conscious decisions were made that put the person on the path to homosexuality.

Ex-gay authors Davies and Rentzel acknowledge this possibility: "Many gays and lesbians believe that they were born homosexual. They do not remember making a *conscious choice* to be sexually drawn to members of their own sex; so, common logic says homosexuality must be genetic or hormonal, and there is nothing that can be done about it."[18] However, individual response to such attractions or inclinations is a matter of choice.

Neurological Conditioning

It is popularly assumed that the brain and hormones direct our behavior in a one-way, cause and effect manner. The brain affects behavior but behavior does not influence (or change) the brain. However, it is apparent from many human and animal studies that behavior can modify the neurons and biochemistry of the brain.[19] The ability of experience to modify brain structure is a well established fact in biology.[20]

The plasticity (i.e., flexibility) of the human brain is greater than most believe. Greenough and colleagues explained, "There is little question that the cerebral cortex and also the cerebella cortex retain the capacity to form new synaptic connections in response to new experience."[21] Environmental stimulation can create a "dynamic synapse-formation process,"[22] meaning new neurons are formed and new interconnections between nerve cells are made. In his book *Blaming the Brain*, Valenstein makes a powerful argument that experience can modify the brain:

> A person's mental state and experience can modify the brain ... Various experiences can cause structural and functional changes in the brain ... Genes are responsible for establishing the scaffolding of the brain, but a large amount of the neuronal growth that leads to the establishment of connections has been shown to be influenced by experience.[23]

The point is this: if choice plays a role in the homosexual condition, then immersion in the gay lifestyle may alter the neural pathways and body chemistry to reinforce homosexual thinking and behavior. If this is the case, then later transformation to heterosexuality would be difficult. Reorientation is possible but it likely requires enormous personal effort and the help of others.[24]

Choice for Lesbians?

In many essays and research reports on lesbianism, choice is acknowledged as an important determinant of homosexual behavior but this finding is never reported in mainstream media.[25] For example, in a 1995 survey in the popular gay magazine *The Advocate*, only 50% of lesbians thought they were born gay, the remainder thought that childhood experiences, personal choice, or both, accounted for their sexual orientation.[26]

Kirkpatrick found that, prior to the onset of stable lesbian coupling, most women in her clinical work reported a "durable" and satisfactory heterosexual marriage.[27] According to Rosik, the literature demonstrates "the relative malleability of erotic attraction for lesbians." Furthermore Rosik states that "studies have reported a 31% to 50% of lesbians consider their sexual orientation to be the result of a conscious, deliberate choice."[28] Now if there is evidence for choice by lesbians, is there evidence of choice for gay men?

Choice for Gay Men?

If homosexual behavior is primarily due to socialization, experience and learning, then there should be evidence that homosexuality can be unlearned, or changed. Fine reviewed much of the literature on change and homosexuality and was surprised to find that regardless of type of treatment (e.g., hypnosis, behavior therapy, psychoanalysis, or an educational approach) "a considerable percentage of overt homosexuals became heterosexual ... If patients are motivated, whatever procedure is adopted a large percentage will give up their homosexuality."[29] In a more recent article, Throckmorton concluded that his review of existing research "contradicts the polices of major mental health organizations because it suggests that sexual orientation, once thought to be an unchanging sexual trait, is actually quite flexible for many people, changing as a result of therapy for some, ministry for others, and spontaneously for still others."[30]

MacIntosh asked 422 psychiatrists if they had helped homosexuals who wanted to change their sexual orientation. Of those responding (the sample size was 285), the doctors said that 23% of their patients had transitioned successfully to heterosexuality, and 84% made significant improvement toward a heterosexual identity.[31] Nicolosi, Byrd, and Potts surveyed 882 individuals who had gone through some type of education or therapy (mostly in religious settings) and as a result experienced some degree of sexual-orientation change. Thirty-four percent reported a significant change away from homosexuality and toward heterosexuality, 43% reported a slight change toward heterosexuality, and 23% reported no change from homosexuality to heterosexuality. In the total group, only 7% said they were ⌐ more psychosocial problems due to therapy.[32]

Robinson interviewed seven married men who had at one time be⌐ heavily involved in homosexual activity and considered themselves to be gay. At the time of the interview, these men, reactivated into religious worship, said they had not participated in homosexual activities for at least one year and were no longer troubled by compulsive sexual thoughts or homosexual desires or fantasies. Robinson summarized his findings:

> The most important conclusion of this study is that change is possible. Participants provided extensive and credible descriptions indicating that they had experienced profound and life altering change. This change included, but was not limited to, a dramatic reduction in frequency, intensity, and duration of homosexual desires ... The change was experienced as being personally fulfilling and greatly increasing the quality of their lives socially, emotionally and spiritually. It would be difficult to argue from the accounts given by these men that the change they reported was imagined, misinterpreted by them, or fundamentally unhealthy.[33]

Psychiatrist Robert L. Spitzer, a leading member of the American Psychiatric Association who helped remove homosexuality from the Association's *Manual of Mental Disorders* in 1973, also believes that some people can change. In 2000, Dr. Spitzer interviewed 200 men and women who claimed to have come out of homosexuality. Spitzer concluded,

> Like most psychiatrists, I thought that homosexual behavior could be resisted—but no one could really change their sexual orientation. I now believe that's untrue—some people can and do change ... Contrary to conventional wisdom, some highly motivated individuals, using a variety of change efforts, can make substantial change in multiple indicators of sexual orientation, and achieve good heterosexual functioning.[34]

Spitzer data suggests some gay men and lesbians were able to change identity, and were able to modify core features of sexual orientation including homoerotic fantasies.[35] What's particularly interesting about this study is that Spitzer made his data available for others to examine. Dr. Scott Hershberger, an essentialist (scientist who believes that homosexuality is biologically determined), elected not only to review Spitzer's data but to conduct a further analysis of the data. Hershberger concluded: "The orderly, law-like pattern of changes in homosexual sexual behavior, homosexual self-identification, and homosexual attraction and fantasy observed in Spitzer's study is strong evidence that reparative therapy can assist individuals in changing their homosexual orientation to a heterosexual orientation."[36]

Stanton Jones and Mark Yarhouse completed a comprehensive longitudinal study of 98 men who participated in a Christian educational approach to overcoming homosexuality. They found 38% of the men had reoriented their lives to heterosexuality or had stopped homosexual behaviors. Also, they found no evidence that the educational and therapeutic intervention had any adverse effects upon the men, including those who did not change their sexual preference. With evidence from many scientific studies, it appears that some self-identified homosexuals have changed their sexual preference and function successfully as heterosexuals.[37]

Agency Exists and Change is Possible

Sexual reorientation is very controversial and many scientists believe it is impossible to change from homosexuality to heterosexuality because sexual preference is biologically determined. But there is too much evidence of reorientation to heterosexuality to dismiss all of the data and personal accounts as lies, fabrications, or poor quality research.[38] Some homosexuals have changed their thinking, feeling, and behavior and have reoriented their lives to heterosexual living.[39] They marry, have children, and believe themselves to be heterosexual—and the transformation appears to be lasting.[40]

Edward Stein, a law school professor, in his 1999 book "*Mismeasure of Desire: The Science, Theory and Ethics of Sexual Orientation*", refutes the role of agency in homosexuality.[41] These are his reasons:

> *1. Introspection.* If you ask men and women who are heterosexual if they chose their sexual disposition and desire, they will almost unanimously say "No." They believe the feelings have always been there. "It's just the way I am." Ergo, homosexuals feel the same way: It's not chosen.
>
> *2. Observation.* Homosexuals, who want to change, and have tried to do so using medication, therapy, support groups, or prayer, have been unable to do so. "Most people who have tried

to change their sexual orientations have failed, [and this] seems to count against voluntarism [agency] in sexual orientation."[42]

3. Intuition. If you are heterosexual, imagine trying to change your own sexual preference—not just your outward behavior but also your underlying desires regarding same-sex sex. If you believe this is impossible, then sexual orientation is determined not chosen.

4. Common Sense. Why would anyone choose a behavior that is stigmatized by society? It doesn't make sense to do something that most people find at best unnatural and at worst disgusting and immoral.

Stein concludes his case that "voluntarism [i.e., agency] in sexual orientation is improbable and the most plausible theories of sexual orientation [assert] that choice does not play a role."[43] Stein's conclusions sound reasonable on the surface, but each has a flaw.

Consider Stein's first point that homosexuality is not a choice because most homosexuals have early memories of feeling different. If childhood trauma (e.g., incest, defensive detachment, sexual abuse) sets the stage for homosexuality, it would be impossible to figure out later in life why one felt different at a young age. Dailey simply states, "Feelings are not proof that homosexuality is inborn."[44] Also, as adults it is impossible to accurately remember feelings one had at age 5 or 6. Adult experience tends to distort the past, and a true remembrance of childhood feelings is nearly impossible for most people.

Second, Stein contends there is no credible proof that people can change their sexual preference. But there is ample evidence that some individuals have reoriented their lives to heterosexual marriage and family life. Research with lesbians demonstrates unequivocally that some women who had previously functioned adequately in heterosexual marriage chose a new lesbian identity. In their new book, entitled *Ex-Gays?*, Stanton Jones and Mark Yarhouse provide convincing evidence that change is possible.[45]

Third, Stein's "Intuition" argument—that you can't just decide to be gay—is refuted by many lesbians who admit to choosing homosexuality for personal, social, or political reasons. Stein adds a challenge to his argument. He suggests that if you are heterosexual and can't imagine being gay, then there is no choice! Unfortunately, the authors realize that some individuals could do many deviant things given the "wrong" environmental experiences. Some could hire a prostitute for sex. Others could buy and sell illicit drugs. A few might spend all their money at a casino. Certainly, there are a few individuals who can imagine participating in homosexual behavior.

Stein's last argument is that no one in his right mind would choose homosexuality because of the negative social consequences. It is quite evident, however, that many people do immoral activities (e.g. steal, lie, murder, rape, embezzle) that are stigmatized and condemned by society. Why they do these things is not easily answered, but it is a fact that many people choose immoral, illegal, and unethical actions. In sum, Stein's arguments are superficial and flawed. His opinion does nothing to refute the role of agency and choice in homosexuality.[46]

We surmise that Stein and many gay and lesbian mental health professionals and academic researchers refuse to recognize moral agency because of their bias that biology absolutely determines sexual orientation. They are desperate to convince every fair and right thinking person that homosexual behavior is beyond one's control. If this were true, then no one would be responsible for his or her behavior, no one would be expected to change, and eventually prejudice against homosexuality would cease because it would be considered an inborn trait like skin color.

CHAPTER FIVE
A NEW THEORY OF HOMOSEXUALITY

We propose that environmental facts, moral agency, and possibly some biological processes contribute to homosexuality. King explains:

> Most researchers today agree that biological and social influences both contribute to the development of sexual orientation. The question is no longer nature versus nurture, but to what extent each influences orientation. They certainly interact in some complex yet undetermined manner. At the moment, the most we can say for biological factors is that they probably predispose (this is not the same as cause) an individual to a particular sexual orientation. What this means is that given a certain genetic background and a particular set of social and environmental influences; it is more likely than not that a person will assume a heterosexual or homosexual orientation.[1]

If all three factors (e.g., environment, agency, and biology) interact, then the question remains: What is the relative contribution of each factor to a homosexual outcome? In other words, is homosexuality mostly due to biology, with some environmental influences and little free will? Or is homosexuality mostly a choice, made more likely due to a pathological family, sexual abuse, a promiscuous peer group, and a genetic predisposition toward shyness, sensitivity, and nonaggression? An illustration of the multiple causality of homosexuality was described by Schmidt:

> A boy with a biological disposition to gender non-conforming behavior is born in a confused culture that associates such

behavior with homosexuality. The boy has a dysfunctional family in which the mother is overwhelming and the father is ineffectual. The boy grows up with no more moral training than is necessary to keep him out of trouble at home or at school. He experiments with homosexual relations as an adolescent and finds pleasure and companionship. As he enters adulthood, he chooses to move to a large city where he can build a life within the homosexual subculture.[2]

Perhaps an analogy may help illustrate our interactional theory. Nicolosi provides comparison between the development of obesity and homosexuality.

> Your son Jack is born with a gene that makes it likely he will gain weight. You really love to cook for him, and so he grows up loving desserts and fried foods. At school he is teased, excluded, and called names, and so he goes home and comforts himself the way he knows best—by eating. 'Maybe they're right', Jack decides, 'Maybe this is who I am'. Pretty soon Jack is overweight and his doctor gives him a note excluding him from physical education class.
>
> "Is 'fat' who he really is? He got that way through a combination of biological factors, parental influence, social influence from peers, and behavioral choice. Just as with homosexuality. Yet as much as overeating may be understandable for Jack (and it feels pretty normal to him), we still recognize that obesity is not healthy."[3]

This account reveals that Jack's obesity is a result of nature, nurture, and choice. He inherited a tendency to be overweight. His diet and home life facilitated his over-eating. The cruelties of his peers lead Jack to assuage his rejection and depression with food. Jack, himself, made decisions to lead a "couch potato" lifestyle. In his mind, Jack would not recognize or admit that he chose his condition. He would say that obesity just happened to him—it was part of who he was and he can't be blamed for that.

Three Models

In Figure 1, we propose multiple pathways for the development of homosexuality. A triangular shape was chosen because it conveys visually the relative contribution of each contributing factor to the whole. The larger the polygon sections of the triangle, the greater its influence in eliciting a homosexual outcome. In addition, the vertical placement of the factors conveys the idea that factors higher up in the triangle can trump those below it. However, factors can free-float, moving up and down much like the blobs in a lava lamp that rise and fall, depending on time and other environmental or health conditions. For example, a person may lose his or her freedom to resist homosexual behavior as time and conditioning reinforce the patterns of homosexual behavior.

Please note that when we use the term *genes* as a contributing factor we are not referring to biology as a direct, causative agent in homosexuality. When we say genes we mean genetically based physical or personality traits that may influence a person's temperament and social interaction. This could in turn lead to opportunities for homosexual socialization and interaction. Genes are NOT posited to be a direct cause of homosexual behavior.

Caution: the three models are simplistic examples of the factors, forces, and conditions that may contribute to a preference for same-sex partners. But the final outcome—homosexuality—cannot be reduced to the simple presence or absence of any of these factors. There may be other influences not yet identified that may be influential. The models will only show how various forces and factors may interact to encourage homosexuality. The case studies presented below are fictional (See models on the next page).

MODEL-A

Abby always considered herself a tomboy. As a child she rejected dolls and dresses and preferred the rough-and-tumble play with boys. She had few girl friends. Abby had a cold, distant father and weak, passive mother. She did not want to grow up and be like her mother—submissive and powerless. Her father was a truck driver, rarely around. At fifteen, Abby was seduced and raped by a boy from school and then emotionally abandoned by him. She grew to distrust men and had no interest in dating other guys. Her closest confidante was her aunt, a longtime lesbian. She also had a gay first cousin in a neighboring town who lived with his partner.

During a stressful time in her senior year of high school, Abby became attracted to a compassionate girlfriend. She confided in a gay-friendly school counselor and was encouraged to explore her homosexual feelings. During this time Abby would occasionally masturbate while watching pornographic videos. Her friend gave her Chastity Bono's memoir (i.e., daughter of

Figure 1: Three Models of Homosexuality

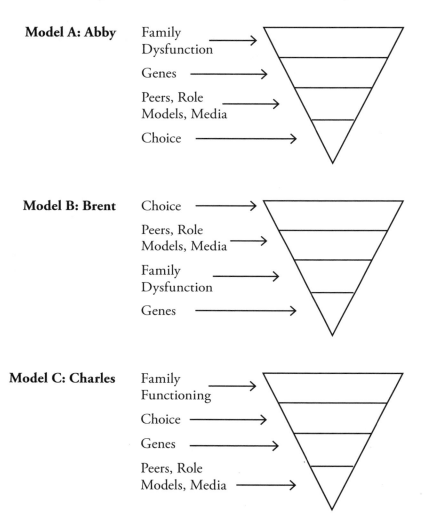

Model A: Abby
Family Dysfunction
Genes
Peers, Role Models, Media
Choice

Model B: Brent
Choice
Peers, Role Models, Media
Family Dysfunction
Genes

Model C: Charles
Family Functioning
Choice
Genes
Peers, Role Models, Media

Cher), *Family Outing*, to read. It is a coming-of-age story of Bono's lesbian experience. Abby followed that up by reading *Early Embraces*, by Lindsey Elder, and *Skin Deep*, edited by Nicole Foster—all true stories of lesbian sexual experiences. After months of sexual frustration, Abby persuaded her girlfriend to have sex.

MODEL-B

Brent's father was a straight-laced minister, warm but strict and judgmental. His relationship with his dad was at times conflicting. He felt he could never measure up to his father's expectations. Brent's parents had a relatively happy and stable marriage, but he could sense that his mother chafed at the father's strong patriarchal control. Rebellion came easy to Brent. In small ways he defied his father and spurned his mother's guidance and love.

During middle childhood and into adolescence, Brent engaged in masturbation and mutual masturbation with his male buddies. He also tried out heterosexual intercourse on several occasions and found it satisfying. As a teen Brent was involved with a punk-rock band whose members experimented with drugs and deviant sexual behaviors. During his last two years of high school Brent hung out with a friend who was gay. Occasionally, the two of them would sneak into a gay bar, drink, socialize, and then have bathroom sex with older men. Brent wasn't sure if he was straight, gay, or bisexual, but he chose to run with the gay crowd for the present.

MODEL-C

Charles had what he considered a normal childhood. His parents were affectionate and available, but they took a laissez-faire approach to parenting. There were few rules and regulations. His parents gave him little moral guidance and direction, and for the most part, Charles was left to make his own decisions. His parents held liberal values regarding sex and sexuality, were openly accepting of alternative lifestyles, and had several gay friends. They gave no direct guidance to Charles on appropriate sexual behavior. Charles recalled that in his early years he felt different somehow but wasn't sure why. He was kind, sensitive, and talented in the arts.

His friends at school were mostly girls who shared his interest in music and drama; he felt comfortable and safe with them. Charles was ill at ease around boys, yet he was attracted to them. He idolized his male teachers and his male cousins, who were tough, rugged men. Charles longed for their attention and affection. Occasionally, he would fantasize about being gay, but the guilt upset him and the fear of homosexuality depressed him. He finally decided to discuss his feelings with a gay student he knew and eventually had sex with this same boy.

These three models acknowledge the possible influence of psychosocial factors and biology, yet they recognize that agency—the freedom to make choices—plays an important part in the process.

Abby, Brent, and Charles represent different pathways to similar, though not identical, ends. They experience homosexuality differently because they have different histories, motivations, and emotional and social conditioning.

Similar Background, But Different Outcome

We realize that there are some youth—for example, let's call one such fellow Harry—who have had a life story similar to Abby, Brent, or Charles, and yet turned out to be heterosexual. So how can we explain this?

An answer is that with Harry, those conditions that might tilt him toward homosexuality existed in different proportions and in a different temporal sequence than for Abby, Brent, and Charles. Like Abby or Charles, Harry was exposed to pornography and liberal sexual mores in the home, but he spent much of his time at a friend's home where heterosexuality was expected. In addition, Harry was more resilient to stress and family dysfunction than was Brent. And last, Harry's moral agency—his freedom to choose—was a more potent factor in influencing sexual attraction. So in the end, Harry met Sally and is heterosexual, while Abby and Charles are homosexual, and Brent is bisexual.

Remember that these models are simplified. The development of homosexuality is more intricate and complicated than these examples. Our scenarios, however, may represent probable pathways to homosexual outcomes. Also note that not every factor need be present to produce a homosexual outcome, and not every factor has the same weight or influence on the development of homosexuality.[4] One individual may be more or less affected by a neglectful father, while another may be more or less traumatized by sexual abuse, while a third person may be more or less influenced by sexually promiscuous peers and the media.

Also, we do not believe that at some discrete point in time, a person "chooses" to be gay. The process of homosexual development is not nearly that clear cut and straightforward. It is likely, however, that at various times along the way to self-identification as homosexual, the individual chooses or attends to feelings, ideas, or behaviors that help move him further along the path to homosexuality. Those contributing factors may change over time—with each factor becoming more (or less) important, depending upon age and other situational conditions—and during that period, the person's sexual preference may flow toward, or away from, a homosexual orientation. During this time of flux and instability we believe that homosexual behavior can be changed and a person can be reoriented toward heterosexual functioning more easily.

CHAPTER SIX
PRACTICAL ADVICE
FOR PARENTS

Before we proceed with the practical applications of our thesis, let us summarize what we have said thus far. First, we believe that heterosexuality is the natural and normal human sexual preference. However, for some individuals this normal neural process is short-circuited and something goes awry. For some individuals sexual preference becomes malleable (i.e., flexible, impressionable) and is able to be swayed by environmental forces and agency (i.e., choice). Second, it is our contention that actions can be taken to support and encourage a heterosexual orientation in children who have sexual-preference uncertainty or are involved in homosexual behavior. We believe that for some children, "guidance along the way [may be] necessary for the process [of heterosexual preference] to work out satisfactorily."[1]

Our parenting recommendations are gleaned from the theories and research presented in chapter 3, and from our own Christian beliefs. In Figure 2, "Family Influences on Child's Sexual Preference," there are three theories on the far left (Psychoanalytic, Social Learning, and Christian Family), and each theory leads to two or more interventions (represented by the seven rectangular boxes in the middle of the diagram). We believe these seven interventions will influence the child's heterosexual preference (the large rectangle on the far right). We will discuss each of the seven interventions in the order they are depicted in Figure 2.

At the end of this section we will briefly outline warning signs of pre-homosexuality where psychotherapy may be warranted. But we will not discuss therapy for a child with gender identity confusion and homosexual inclinations, nor will we provide a description of reorientation therapy for those who want to change their sexual preference. There are many resources available on these topics.[2] An excellent resource for parents who want more detailed information can be found in Joseph and Linda Nicolosi's book, *"A Parent's Guide to Preventing Homosexuality"*.

Figure 2: Family Influences on a Child's Sexual Preference

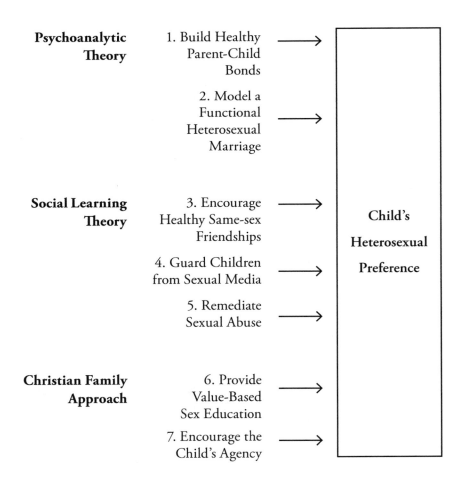

Seven Suggestions for Fostering Heterosexuality

1. BUILD HEALTHY PARENT-CHILD RELATIONSHIPS

One psychological theory suggests that a cold, rejecting father, and an over involved and excessively sympathetic mother may predispose a male child to homosexual behavior.[3] The opposite parent characteristics may prevent homosexuality. This has implications for both fathers and mothers.

Advice to fathers helping sons. Dr. Joseph Nicolosi, who has counseled many men out of homosexuality, asserts that boys need *salient* fathers: "Salient means two things: strong and also benevolent. A child needs to see you as confident, self-assured, and decisive. But he also needs to see you as supportive, sensitive, and caring."[4] If fathers provide appropriate affection, attention, and support to sons, then sons will respect, emulate, and identify with fathers. Sons will develop a masculine gender identity. After working with many homosexuals, psychoanalyst Dr. Irving Bieber said he has never met "a male homosexual whose father openly loved and respected him."[5] He concluded that "a constructive, warmly supportive father *precludes the possibility* of a homosexual son."[6]

Please note that some fathers think they are warm and supportive but are not, just like some husbands believe they treat their wives with respect and equality but fail to do so. It is unfortunate that many people do not perceive their own faults and rarely evaluate their own inadequacies. Thus, some fathers may need critical but encouraging feedback from wives, from brothers or sisters, or from a professional counselor to see their fathering behavior for what it truly is and to change for the better. The Lord has made it clear that those who are humble and seek God's guidance can perceive their sins (i.e., and the hurt or harm they do to others), make improvements and eventually become "strong" in areas of previous weakness.

Second, fathers may want to help sons become at least minimally proficient in one physical activity. This could include soccer, bowling, football, swimming, skateboarding, wrestling, karate, or scouting. A boy does *not* need to be an athlete to develop a heterosexual identity, but it may be helpful if a boy displays some sports skills. Cruel peers may make fun of a boy who is uncoordinated and fearful of rough-and-tumble play. As Fitzgibbons points out, "In a sports oriented culture like our own, if a young boy is unable to throw, catch, or kick a ball, he is likely to be excluded, isolated and ridiculed."[7] A father may have to work harder with a less active, uncoordinated, or artistic son. Alan Medinger's warns of this situation:

> If a boy is born slight of build, poorly coordinated, and without a typical male right-brain visual-spatial specialization, then he is apt to do poorly in the activities that prompt affirmation [of his manhood] from men and other boys. If he is born with a passive rather than aggressive nature, the first experience of rejection may send him into withdrawal from the world of men rather than lead him to try harder.[8]

But fathers need not go overboard in sports and should not force a son into athletics, especially if the son lacks the talent or disposition. Sports are only one way (but a good way) for fathers to affirm masculinity in their sons. Affirmation can also occur when a son cares for younger siblings, receives a Boy Scout award, or wins the school reading contest.

Third, fathers must give special attention to a "sensitive son." Such a child has also been called "effeminate" or given the pejorative label of "sissy boy." This child is likely to display "gender atypical" behaviors, e.g., playing with dolls, dressing in girl clothes, and he may show little interest in active, occasionally aggressive play common among young boys. Gender nonconformity in early childhood is often associated with later homosexual identity and behavior.[9] Such behavior is an early warning sign that this boy needs special attention from his father.

The sensitive boy is especially susceptible to the emotional feelings flowing within the family system. He is finely attuned to negative feelings and is easily hurt by shame, ridicule, or even mild rebuke. Criticism (e.g. "You need to grow up and be man!"), even well-intentioned, is taken to heart. The child's strong feelings may be evident, not in outward behavior, but in more subtle signs of moodiness that can range from quiet withdrawal to outbursts of destructive action. With a sensitive son, a father can make a determined effort to share feelings about what is going on in the family system. The father can help his son identify and manage both positive and negative emotional states.

Look for ways to build up and reinforce the boy's masculinity. Include him in your activities and in your associations with other male role models. Do not leave him out or leave him behind even if he is somewhat hesitant to join in. When you tackle jobs like changing the car oil, mowing the lawn, fixing the toilet, shoveling the snow, or building the birdhouse, get your son involved. On a regular schedule, take your sensitive son on special "father-son" outings that you both enjoy such as a trip to a museum, a movie, a hike in the woods, rafting on a river, dinner at his favorite fast food joint, or playing soccer in the park. A sensitive son may be helped by the companionship of a pet, especially a dog that can be a regular buddy and affectionate friend.

In summary, a father should not worry if such a child occasionally displays gender-atypical activities such as cross-dressing, playing with dolls, or trying on mom's jewelry. This is normal if not carried to excess (see endnote 1 for the warning signs that may require early intervention). The problem is not that the child has some feminine traits but that his masculine characteristics need bolstering.[10] Thus, a father should not rebuff the shy, sensitive, musical, or artistic son. "Every boy," Nicolosi advises, "has a deep longing to be held, to be loved by a father figure, to be mentored into the world of men, and to have his masculine nature affirmed."[11]

Fathers helping daughters. Many scholars believe a daughter's gender identity is greatly influenced by the presence of a warm, supportive, and affectionate father.[12] Fathers should love their daughters and show them appropriate physical affection. But any type of sexual abuse can be devastating and may misdirect the natural and normal development of a heterosexual orientation. Jeanette Howard, an ex-lesbian, suggests that "one of the father's main roles is to affirm his daughter in her femininity ... His opinion of his daughter provides affirmation or disapproval in a way that a mother cannot. ... Dad can bring confidence into his daughter's sense of feminine identity."[13] If a daughter feels safe, secure, and protected by her father, then she can later transfer these feelings into adult heterosexual relationships.

Advice for mothers helping sons. Mothers should develop warm, affectionate, and nurturing relationships with sons. A boy's closeness to his mother also fosters his masculinity. Mothers should give love and kindness but must not pamper or mollycoddle sons. They should remember that many homosexual men report mothers who were overprotective and too sympathetic. When a son is injured, frightened, or weak, it is the mother's job to find the balance between cuddling compassion and providing a tough, detached, encouragement that will allow him to face his fears, pain, and discomfort.

With a son, a mother must learn to tolerate typical boy behaviors: running, jumping, fighting, and getting into things. Within limits, he should be allowed to get dirty and to rough-house. These are natural proclivities for his gender. Of course, the mother must set limits and redirect destructive play, but boys play differently than girls and a mother may need to tolerate more aggressive attitudes and actions from sons. A mother might prefer the quiet demeanor and nondestructive play of a little daughter but she needs to resist the thought and take joy in a son's energy and activity.

Mothers should not favor a son over his father even if the son is more responsive and compassionate than the husband. If mothers do this, sons may identify with the mother (i.e., emulate and model after) and not bond with the father.[14] Joseph Nicolosi explains, "If a mother has no emotionally secure relationship with a man, she may unconsciously seek to satisfy her emotional needs with her son, maintaining an unhealthy, overly intimate connection that may seemingly meet her own needs but that will not be in the best interest of her son."[15] Even if there are marital problems, a mother should not turn to a sympathetic son to meet her intimacy needs.

Divorced or never-married women may have had bad experiences with men; men who were brutal, controlling, and unfeeling. In such a case, a mother must refrain from demeaning and disparaging all men ("men are so callous," "men are stupid," etc.) If a mother does this, she may undermine her son's masculinity. Moms please note: single parenting does not increase the risk of a son becoming homosexual. It has more to do with how the mother portrays men and how she fosters her son's masculinity.

In other families, the father may be physically present but psychologically absent. The father is detached and uninvolved. This presents an even bigger challenge for a mother. She must try to stay positive about men in general—and project that to her son—even when there is an incompetent and ineffectual father in the home. There is no quick and easy fix to such a situation. All a mother can do is to support her son's masculinity and let go of her anger and disappointment in her husband. This is not a great solution but may be the best that can be achieved.

Mothers helping daughters. There is much less research on the development of homosexuality in girls than there is on boys. Thus, there is less information from which to glean practical advice on reducing the risk of homosexual behavior in daughters. Nevertheless, defensive detachment (i.e., rejection of and hostility to the mother) can occur with daughters as it does between fathers and sons. Worthen and Davies, who have counseled many women with homosexual attractions, found that "the lesbian daughter often senses something missing in her relationship with her mother. The little girl grows up without a true sense of nurturing. For a multitude of reasons, she and her mother don't make a strong emotional connection. So the daughter begins an unconscious search for a woman to nurture her."[16]

Worthen and Davies continue, "Many lesbians see their mothers as weak, ineffectual and unaffirming of their daughter's femininity ... The mother's passive [behavior] can give the daughter wrong ideas about a wife's role in the home. The young girl may think, 'If that's what being a woman is all about, I don't want any part of it."[17] The implication of this finding is obvious: mothers must lovingly nurture their daughters as well as model femininity, psychological strength, and practical competence in daily life. If the mother is passive, withdrawn, or depressed, the daughter may not identify with her and this will hamper the daughter's gender identity development and may influence her sexual orientation.[18]

A mother can also strengthen the heterosexual preference of daughters by the demonstrating a loving relationship with her husband. Girls' sexual identity and their sexual preference are modeled after the parent's marital relationship. If the parents are comfortable and happy with their marriage and their masculine and feminine roles, then the daughter is more likely to development a normal gender identity and heterosexual preference.[19]

A parallel to the "sensitive son" is the "tomboy daughter". As previously noted for boys, some girls may also display "gender atypical" behaviors at an early age. Physical activity and sports may be more interesting than tea-parties, stuffed animals, and playing house. Such daughters may shun dolls and dresses and prefer to climb trees, throw rocks, and rough-house with boys. As she grows up, she may prefer jeans and tennis shoes to dresses and heels. Though research has shown that many lesbians were tomboys in their youth, very few typical tomboys become lesbian.[20]

However, if masculine behaviors and male attitudes predominate and are disruptive to family life, the daughter may need special attention to encourage the feminine side of her personality and behavior. As suggested for fathers of sensitive sons, mothers of tomboys can spend extra time and effort to encourage their daughter's femininity. There is no magical cure: just close proximity, lots of talking, and spending time in enjoyable mother-daughter activities. However, if the girl communicates persistent, severe distress or disgust with her feminine body or her gender identity then therapy is warranted.

2. CREATE A HAPPY MARRIAGE

In general, a happy and healthy marriage has a salutary influence on the sexual orientation of children. A couple who shows love and respect in marriage presents a powerful model of traditional gender identification and heterosexuality. But this does not mean that husbands and wives must be completely traditional in their own lives. For example, the wife may be the athlete and a civil engineer while the father may be a musician who cannot throw a spiral pass. The spouses in this case display somewhat gender atypical behaviors, but this is no cause for alarm. What makes the difference in the child's development of a heterosexual preference is the fact that the spouses love one another and are comfortable and confident in their respective feminine and masculine roles.[21] If parents would live a "normal and happy heterosexual married life," very few children would be attracted to homosexuality.[22]

The impact of a dysfunctional marriage on a child's sexual preference is articulated by ex-lesbian Jeanette Howard:

> How a child sees her parents relating has a lasting impact. If they fail to show affection and attention toward each other, the daughter soon picks up on their subliminal messages. If the mother is critical and disrespectful of her husband, the daughter may accept that as the normal and correct attitude to have toward all men. If the mother is downtrodden and weak, the girl might reject anything feminine as being second class and not worth embracing. If the father is abusive to his wife, the little girl may soon learn not to trust men, and will possibly find ways to live without them. If the father leaves his pornography around the house, or leers at the women on television, the child deduces that men "only want one thing," and she may detach herself from any emotionally intimate relating with men.[23]

Thus, it is the influence of a loving and affectionate married couple that will help insulate any child from the forces of promiscuity and from a desire to experiment with homosexual behavior. Parents should not underestimate the power of marital love in making a child more less vulnerable to variety of sexual deviations.

3. ENCOURAGE HEALTHY SAME-SEX FRIENDSHIPS IN CHILDHOOD

Therapist Joseph Nicolosi warns, "Same-sex peers are among the most important influences in your son's life. Male friends are key factors in masculine gender formation and future heterosexual development"[24] It is important to encourage your child's interaction with same-sex friends: boys with boys, and girls with girls. Peers are powerful socializing agents. The child's peers help to direct him or her into traditional gender identity and gender roles. Boys bring out the boyish nature in boys, and girl friends elicit feminine thinking and behavior in girls. At times, and in certain places, it may be difficult to find appropriate playmates for your children. It may take time and money driving many miles to find a friend for your son or daughter. Opposite-sex friends are appropriate too, but not to the complete exclusion of same-sex peers. Growing up with close same-sex friends will strengthen a child's gender identity and promote a heterosexual preference.

When the children get together to play, facilitate gender-typical activities. We are not suggesting you limit your children to stereotypical boy and girl play! And, of course, there are some things that both boys and girls like to do: build a fort, climb a tree, fly a kite, use Lego blocks, swim at the pool, or kick a soccer ball. You can, however, direct some traditional play activities. For example, you might help the boys play baseball, ride bikes, or have a water fight. You could plan a tea party, play dress-up, or make jewelry with your daughters and her friends. But don't get carried away in directing stereotypical activities. Most of the time you won't need to worry about planning play activities, but in some cases you may need to be more directive in encouraging gender-typical play behaviors.

During the teenage years managing your adolescent's social relationships is different. Parents have much less control, and at times all you can do is cross your fingers and hope for the best. You hope your teen will choose peers with values similar to your own, and you hope your teen will engage in wholesome, non-sexual activities. One way to help with this is to communicate your sexual values gently and clearly, and provide appropriate sex education, over the course of the child's life. At this stage, the teen should have a mix of both male and female friends. Some encouragement of opposite-sex interactions is appropriate if monitored or chaperoned. Group dating is probably the best method of mixed gender socialization since it normally avoids the temptation and pressure of sexual intimacy. This is particularly important to have as a ground rule before your teen reaches the age of 16.

One caution: if there is concern about the sexual orientation of a teenager, early dating is not endorsed by these authors. Teenage single dating and tacit approval of premarital sex is *not* a recommended strategy to ensure a teen's heterosexuality! Untimely premarital sexual experience will not solve the problem of homosexuality but will only confuse matters. Inappropriate sexual experience encourages more improper sexual experimentation.

4. GUARD YOUR CHILDREN FROM SEXUALIZATION BY THE MEDIA

Popular media (music, television, DVDs, the Internet, and teen magazines) will attract and tempt youth into premature sexual thoughts, feelings, and behaviors.[25] The "sexualization" of our children by the media makes a child (or youth) seem sensual and sexy and ready and willing to engage in sexual behaviors at young ages. American media saturate youth culture with sexual images, sounds, and feelings, portraying heterosexual or homosexual sex as attractive options. The culprits include Hollywood producers, movie stars, advertising agencies, fashion designers, magazine editors, and rock musicians.

Sexualization leads to experimentation of sexual thoughts, sexual identities, and sexual behaviors. Parents need to reduce child sexualization and by so doing parents will decrease the likelihood that their children will engage in premarital sex, heterosexual or homosexual. Here are some suggestions.

1. Teach and model modesty in dress and fashion. Discourage or forbid early use of make-up, earrings, and other jewelry that can make a child appear older and more mature. Feminine dress should not expose the breasts, thighs, the stomach, or the buttocks. Sloppy, low-rider jeans are not appropriate for boys.

2. Restrict children's viewing of TV, DVDs, music CDs, and Internet Websites that promote sexual immorality. Several TV sitcoms and movies may be viewed as cute and innocent comedies but in reality teach and model lasciviousness and promiscuity that can change thinking, emotions, and even behavior.

3. Expose your children to wholesome and appropriate music, movies, books, and TV early in life. When older the child is more likely to be offended by acts of immorality and reject them.

4. Do not permit early dating or any unchaperoned mixed-sex interaction. Group dating at age sixteen may be permissible, but single dating should not be allowed until age seventeen and that should be limited to once or twice a month.

The popular youth culture that promotes immorality and promiscuity is so potent and powerful that parents must defend against it. Parents cannot stand idly by and hope young children will be unaffected by the sexual wickedness promoted in the media and make good choices on their own. They need restrictions, supervision, and guidance.

5. REMEDIATE SEXUAL ABUSE

Children who have suffered sexual abuse should receive professional assessment and therapy. Sexual abuse derails the normal development of a heterosexual preference.[26] A sexually abused child is more likely to experiment with early sexual behavior and is more likely to question his or her sexual preference. Choose a therapist carefully. A parent should interview the therapist before treatment begins. The goal of therapy should be agreed upon by the parent and therapist.

A minister with a degree in counseling, a master's level social worker, a psychologist, or a marriage and family therapist are all qualified to help in cases of abuse. Sexual abuse, either homosexual or heterosexual, has the potential to confuse a child's gender identity. Such gender confusion is often a factor in derailing a normal heterosexual orientation. Early sexual involvement of any type by young children or teens may misdirect heterosexuality. In either case, a child who was sexually abused or a child who experienced early sexualization should be seen by a professional therapist. Find a religious or secular therapist who has similar values and beliefs regarding the importance of heterosexuality. Dr. James Dobson, a Christian psychologist and founder of *Focus on the Family*, gave this warning:

> If you seek help for your child be careful whom you chose. Most psychiatrists and psychologists would attempt to affirm the child or youth's pre-homosexual tendencies. Be very careful whom you consult. Getting the wrong advice at [an early] stage could be most unfortunate, solidifying the tendencies that are developing. Most secular psychiatrists, psychologist, and counselors would, I believe, take the wrong approach—telling your child that he is homosexual and needs to accept that fact.[27]

6. PROVIDE VALUE-BASED SEX EDUCATION AT HOME

Parents must communicate their sexual values and beliefs directly to their children. They must also provide accurate and timely sex education to their children over many years. Numerous scientific studies have shown that parents do poorly at both of these tasks.[28]

Teach the meaning and value of heterosexuality. Whether or not you are religious, you can teach your children that humans have been designed (by nature or a higher power) for heterosexual living. Men and women complement each other, and together they can create the best environment for raising children. Whether you are Christian, Jew, or Muslim, you can teach your children that God created and blessed the heterosexual family. It is the basis for all civilizations. Gender-role differentiation is part of God's plan. Our masculine and feminine natures make us different yet complementary and compatible. Don't go overboard, but in a variety of ways, depending on your particular religious beliefs and personal values, make a case for the divine creation of husband-wife relationships and the value of some gender-role differentiation between men and women.

It is important to teach your child respect for all people. We live in a diverse, pluralistic society where different worldviews exist. However, teaching tolerance does not mean that we need to celebrate all forms of sexuality. Families who do not value homosexuality can teach their children to respect those who take that path—but teach children not to condone that lifestyle. Respect and tolerance are extended to the *person*; it need not extend to the activities or the lifestyle.

In addition, your children can be taught how to respond to questions or teachings about homosexuality that they will encounter in schools or with friends. *Prepare* <u>and</u> *practice* appropriate non-hurtful, non-judgmental responses that your children can use to comment on or react to questions about homosexuality. Many parents have helped children fashion an assertive, but non-hurtful, response to someone who offers the child alcohol or drugs. Do the same thing here. Work out simple, non-threatening statements in line with your values or religious beliefs. You might ask your teen what he or she would say if someone asked: "What do you think about gays?" or "Are you homophobic?" or "What do you think about lesbians?" Take each statement and practice several appropriate responses until the child or youth understands and is comfortable with a suitable reply.

For example, the teen could respond with these statements: "I don't believe homosexual behavior is right for me, but others may feel differently" or "I think homosexuality is wrong, but you may not agree with me—and that is fine" or "If you are gay, that's your choice; but I am not" or "I think men and women should marry each other, and that's the kind of family I want." Help your teen understand that there is little point in arguing or debating the rightness or wrongness of homosexuality. It's a waste of time and will only hurt or offend others. The teen should be able to sincerely say, "It's okay for you to believe what you want, and it's okay for me to believe what I want."

Provide sex education. In our experience, parents do a poor job in educating their children about sex and sexual morality. Parents are unsure and unprepared to give specific and detailed instruction. They are afraid to take a stand. Some parents may have a good conversation with their child when he or she is 7, 10, or 12, but then never say another word about sex. They assume their child is getting the necessary information somewhere from someone! This is probably true, but it's a bad choice. A dialogue about human sexuality should be opened up with children periodically across many years. "Parents should point out to children that the basic biology of sexuality logically suggests the norm of heterosexuality."[29] Parents can encourage their children to refrain from any kind of intimate sexual behavior prior to marriage. There are many resources for teaching this to children.[30]

Discuss Sexual-Preference Uncertainty. Adolescence is a time of confusion and uncertainty about many things. Erik Erikson, a well-regarded developmental psychologist, called this period of psychosocial conflict the stage of identity formation verses identity confusion. Teens question who they are and what they want to become. They test and try out various ways of thinking and acting.[31] "Through this process, adolescents seek to understand who they are by narrowing down and making choices about their personal, occupational, sexual, and political commitments."[32] Teens ponder their possibilities. "According to Erikson, in complex societies, teenagers experience an identity crisis—a temporary period of confusion and distress as they experiment with alternatives before settling on values and goals."[33]

Fears and doubts about their sexual attractiveness and their sexual attractions are not uncommon for adolescents. As they struggle with identity formation, adolescents are more vulnerable to the influence of friends, teachers, and the media.[34] Some youth may be puzzled by their strong emotional bonds to same-sex friends, and some may experience momentary feelings of same-sex attraction. This is not unusual and is no time for the parents to panic! These facts should be explained to your teenager:

> By itself, deep caring for a person of the same sex is no
> indicator of homosexuality. Parents should not suspect their

child is homosexual merely because of a close friendship with someone of the same sex ... Parents [can] teach their children the distinction between close emotional attachments and sexual relationships.[35]

If your teenager is confused about his or her gender identity (the inner sense of being male or female), or about sexual preference (the object of one's sexual desires), the teen may only share those feelings with a friend, a teacher, or a school counselor. You (the parent) may not even know, and herein lays the danger. These other voices are likely to interpret the teen's confusion as a sign of latent homosexuality and may encourage the teen to explore that possibility of homosexuality. These individuals may fail to consider that the teen is just a confused heterosexual searching for answers and support.

Kathy Mitchell and Marcy Sugar, "advice experts" for the nationally syndicated newspaper column "Annie's Mailbox," recently told parents of a teen with homosexual feelings to accept their son's sexual orientation and to get help from the gay support group PFLAG. The evidence for this recommendation was (1) the parent's description of their son's online chat about gay sex, and (2) his revelation that he didn't have romantic feelings for girls.[36]

Their pseudo-psychological diagnosis might compare to a father (a psychologist for example) telling his daughter that her frequent abdominal pain and cramping was simply PMS. If she was told, "Just accept it, this is who you are—a menstruating female," this would be bad advice from her father. And likewise it's bad advice from Mitchell and Sugar, who are equally unqualified. We consider Mitchell and Sugar's public response irresponsible and reckless. Yet their column is read by millions of Americans and is considered a source of trustworthy information. Few people read professional journals or academic textbooks; therefore, few people have an understanding of the development of sexual preference and the etiology of homosexual behavior. There is good reason why parents should not necessarily believe what they read from "experts." It has become clearer and clearer that many of these so-called experts are not offering their advice based on science but on their worldview, a kind of activism masqueraded as science.

In today's promiscuous and oversexed society some adolescents experience doubt or confusion about sexual preference. Teens may be unsure whether they are attracted to members of the opposite sex, their own sex, or both sexes. This uncertainty is more common today as adolescents are encouraged by peers, parents, and Hollywood to experiment with a variety of sexual identities and behaviors.

Temporary confusion about one's sexual preference, however, is not well understood, nor is it well researched. Parents, pundits (like Mitchell and Sugar) and many mental health professionals seem to take the position that any uncertainty indicates latent homosexuality. They reject the idea that sexual attraction is in any way a choice. The purveyors of political correctness will respond that an individual who experiences homosexual desires needs only enlightened education and encouragement to explore homosexuality. Because mental health professionals (as a group) are biased toward accepting and supporting homosexuality, a counselor may inadvertently miss the opportunity to help a teen affirm his or her heterosexuality.

Some counselors and school personnel would simply interpret sexual-preference uncertainty (remember this is our term, not one used by doctors or psychologists) as anxiety caused by the youth's avoidance or rejection of his or her presumed pre-homosexual longings or his or her internalized homophobia. The teacher or counselor may then encourage the youth to accept homosexual desires as normal and healthy and to explore them.[37] These authority figures may teach, with subtlety, the dominant philosophy of promiscuous sexuality: One is obligated to act upon one's sexual desires without reference to any moral code; the individual alone decides what is right and wrong; and homosexuality is a legitimate expression of one's sexuality. Before the youth or the parents know what is going on, the teen may be given the pamphlet "*Just the Facts*" and be ushered into a gay support group where the youth may be encouraged to explore his or her "emerging homosexuality."[38] All of this can happen without a parent's knowledge or consent.

"*Just the Facts*" is a promotional brochure from the American Psychological Association (and endorsed by all major educational associations) and has been distributed to thousands of public school personnel across the country to "set the record straight" about homosexuality. It states unequivocally that homosexuality is normal and healthy, and that any attempt to change a child's sexual orientation is immoral, unethical, and impossible.[39] This one-sided propaganda by the school, the media, and the medical and psychological communities make it imperative that parents have open and frank discussions with their teens about homosexuality and what the teens should expect to encounter in our gay-affirming culture.

7. TEACHING PERSONAL RESPONSIBILITY: THE ROLE OF AGENCY

Recall that moral agency (choice) is a key component in our theory of homosexuality. Our last advice to parents is to initiate pointed discussions with your children on the role of agency in human behavior. You can explain what agency is and give examples of how youth (and adults) use their agency for positive or negative outcomes. For example, in traditional Christian, Muslim, and Jewish theology, men and women are free to choose right behavior that conforms to God's will, or to choose evil. Something "evil" is innately hurtful to the individual and harmful to society.

With any moral dilemma a choice is available: to choose an action in harmony with God's will or purpose, or to act in opposition or defiance to God's will. Obedience to God's laws leads to serenity and personal growth. Disobedience leads to remorse, guilt, unhappiness, and developmental regression. A teen, for example, can be taught that he may not be able to choose to be a great basketball player (because he is short and uncoordinated), but he can decide to treat a friend with kindness, to tell the truth, and to refrain from non-marital sexual behaviors. These are moral choices.

Sexual urges are natural during adolescence, but premarital sexual behavior (heterosexual or homosexual) is not irresistible and inevitable. A church leader, Boyd K. Packer explains to Christian youth:

> Normal [sexual] desire and attractions emerge in the teenager years; there is the temptation to experiment, to tamper with the sacred power of procreation. These desires can be intensified, even perverted, by pornography, improper music, or the encouragement from unworthy associations. . . [But] the gates of freedom, and the good or bad beyond, swing open or closed to the password *choice*. You are free to choose a path.[40]

Sexual thoughts and behaviors are choices—moral choices. Masturbation, premarital heterosexual sex, and homosexual behavior are subservient to human agency. Dailey commented that "while we all have tendencies or weaknesses, each of us has some capacity to strive against wrong or harmful urges."[41] Agency is the ability and responsibility to make moral choices and will ultimately benefit the individual and society.

Help children understand they are moral agents, able to choose and manage their sexual thinking and behaviors. Youth should know that no predisposing factor (biological or environmental) can override one's freedom to make moral decisions regarding sexual behavior.

If a teen seems confused or uncertain about sexual preference, parents need not criticize, condemn, or shame the child. This approach will only backfire and inflame rebellion or lead to a child's withdrawal and depression. Agency is not fostered by rejection, by censure, or by force. A better approach is presented in Dean Byrd's article in the September 1999 *Ensign* entitled "When a Loved One Struggles with Same-Sex Attraction." He explains ten principles for providing loving support to a family member who struggles with homosexual thoughts and behavior.

SUMMARY OF PARENTING ADVICE

It is important to recap our parenting recommendations to avoid misunderstanding. We believe that heterosexuality develops quite naturally and easily in most children without much direction from parents, but in today's promiscuous society there is some cause for concern. A few children may need extra help to guide them into heterosexuality. We've given the reader specific suggestions how to do this, but the particulars are not as important as the more general principles that underline our ideas. The critical components that will strengthen a child's heterosexual potential are (a) the parents' relatively happy and stable marriage, (b) healthy parent-child relationships, (c) helping the child avoid the evil influences in society that promote sexual promiscuity, and (d) teaching the child true principles of human sexuality and the reality of moral agency. The other specific suggestions are of secondary significance.

Regarding our advice to fathers and mothers (about how to treat a son or daughter), we are worried that you may believe we are promoting rigid gender-stereotypes. We believe that the most well-adjusted children and adults have a healthy mix of both traditional male and female characteristics. But on the other hand, we believe you should not go overboard in promoting *genderless* behavior in your children. Encouraging some gender-specific thinking and acting may foster a traditional heterosexual identity and sexual preference.

Lastly, the reader should be aware that our specific parenting advice has not been empirically tested by research. We cannot tell you there is strong scientific evidence to support our recommendation. Science does not allow us to randomly assign children into experimental and control groups and then expose one group of children to factors that encourage homosexuality and expose the second group to factors that discourage homosexuality and then assess the results in 15 years. Such an experiment would test our recommendations, but it is neither ethical nor practical to do so. Thus, we must make inferences from existing research and theory on homosexuality and from divine truths that God has revealed.

We believe that truth comes not from science alone but also from the revealed word of God through Holy Writ and by personal revelation. This inspiration informs one's conscience about the true nature of our sexuality and proper sexual conduct.

Warning Signs that May Require Intervention

Dr. Joseph Nicolosi, an expert on the treatment of homosexuality, gives five markers for a child with Gender Identity disorder. These signs can be seen in a child as early as two years old, or they may not occur until middle childhood or even early adolescence:

> 1. Repeatedly stated desire to be, or insistence that he or she is, the other sex.
> 2. In boys, preference for cross-dressing, or simulating female attire; and in girls, the insistence on wearing only stereotypical masculine clothing.
> 3. Strong and persistent preference for cross-sexual roles in make-believe play, or persistent fantasies of being the other sex.
> 4. Intense desire to participate in stereotypical games and pastimes of the other sex.
> 5. Strong preference for playmates of the other sex.[42]

These indicators warn the parent that if your son or daughter gets too carried away in cross-gender play or identification with the opposite sex, then intervention may be required to turn the child back to heterosexuality. Extreme effeminate mannerisms in your son or exaggerated tomboyishness in your daughter is a warning sign of Gender Identity confusion. Therapists Rekers and Meed provide an example of Becky (age 8), who was later successfully treated for Gender Identity confusion.

> Becky dressed exclusively in boys' pants and often wore cowboy boots, while consistently rejecting feminine clothing and jewelry. Her only use of feminine cosmetic articles was to draw a moustache and/or a beard on her face. She appeared masculine in her gestures, mannerisms, and walk ... She often projected her voice very low so that she sounded like a man, she

expressed the desire to be a boy, and she adopted male roles in play. She preferred the company of boys and did not interact well with other girls. Her behavior was excessively aggressive.[43]

There are a few other signs that may help identify a child at risk for homosexuality. First, if the child demonstrates (through words or actions) a disdain or discomfort with his or her body, especially the sexual organs, that is cause for concern. The little boy who doesn't want a penis or the young girl who hates to menstruate or tries to suppress breast development—all draw red flags. If the child has been sexually molested, parents should seek psychological assessment and treatment. Sexual abuse seems to confuse or frustrate normal gender identify formation. We should point out that a child born with hermaphrodism (or intersex) will require special medical and psychological treatment in regards to gender identity and sexual preference. A hermaphrodite is a child born with underdeveloped male *and* female sexual organs. Interestingly enough, most intersex children are able to adjust to their constructed gender identity—very few struggle with homosexuality, suggesting that homosexuality is very different from intersex challenges.

We offer some counsel to parents whose children struggle with gender identity and sexual preference issues. First, it is unlikely that parents alone can make major changes in a child's gender identity or sexual preference. Your love and support are needed in a supporting role, but this is not the catalyst for change that is needed. Spiritual counseling and secular based therapy will be required. Parents should interview the religious or secular therapist before allowing their child to be treated. You should be forewarned that most psychologists, social workers, and psychiatrists believe a child's sexual preference should NOT be treated.

They believe that reorientation therapy, that helps a patient give up homosexual behavior, is immoral and unethical.[44] Many condemn the practice as unproductive and psychologically harmful.[45] For example, Stein contends:

> The therapist evaluating a person who is seeking to change his or her sexual orientation is ethically obligated to inform the patient both that homosexuality is not considered officially to be a mental disorder and that there is no valid evidence that change in sexual orientation is possible as a result of psychological intervention. Given these conditions, it is currently ethically

indefensible for a therapist to attempt to change the sexual orientation of a patient.[46]

However, our views support an individual's right to reject a homosexual identity and to get help to change his or her homosexual behavior. And parents certainly have a right to make those choices for their children. Dr. Richard Green, a psychiatrist and lawyer, offers the following conclusion:

> The right of parents to oversee the development of children is a long-established principle. Who is to dictate that parents may not try to raise their children in a manner that maximizes the possibility of a heterosexual outcome? ... Parents have the legal right to seek treatment to modify their child's cross-gender behavior to standard boy or girl behavior, even if their motivation is to prevent homosexuality. If that prerogative is denied, should parents also be denied the right to raise their children as atheists, or as priests?[47]

There are others who support a client's right to treatment. For example, Rosik states that therapists should *not* "prohibit change-orientated therapies," but should respect the religious beliefs and values of clients who want to strengthen their "heterosexual potential."[48] Yarhouse and Throckmorton, well-regarded therapists and academic researchers, also take a positive position on reorientation therapy: "Respect for the autonomy and self-determination of clients, respect for diversity, and existing scientific research, all favor the viability of reorientation therapies and religion-based ministries."[49]

After therapy has begun, parents should have intermittent discussions with the therapist and possibly even request several sessions of family therapy. Parents may want to get permission to observe the therapy behind a one-way mirror, or listen to therapy in another room or from a tape recording. In this way parents monitor the therapy. If the therapist will not let you observe or listen to the therapy session, then find another therapist who will permit this. Parents may need some help as well. Family difficulties may contribute to gender identity confusion in children and insecurity regarding sexual preference.[50] If you want your child to get better, you and your spouse may need to change also—so be open to this idea of marital therapy.

CHAPTER SEVEN
CONCLUSIONS

The Changing Nature of Sexual Morals

Encouraging heterosexuality in a diverse, pluralistic society like America is, unfortunately, a contentious issue.[1] Many psychologists, civil rights workers, gay activists, feminists, media celebrities, and others would vehemently oppose our position and reject our arguments.[2] Yet these critics lionize freedom of speech and revel in diversity of opinion as long as you don't oppose them.[3] Disagreement with their "politically correct views" regarding homosexuality is met with fierce derision and cries of bigotry and homophobia.[4] Our quiet call to encourage heterosexuality would be seen by critics as only slightly less damning than the terrible murder of the young gay man Matthew Shepard who was beaten and left for dead on a fence post in Wyoming.[5]

Yet, for many centuries Jewish, Christian, and Islamic religions have considered homosexuality deviant and injurious to society.[6] About half of the world's population has historically followed these religious traditions. For the past two hundred years, most doctors and mental health professionals concurred. True, there have always been a few (scientists, doctors, playwrights, and artists) who have sought to normalize homosexuality, but it has only been in the past forty years that attitudes have changed dramatically. "In less than a century, many in our society have moved from considering homosexuality a moral evil, to considering it a sickness, to denying that it has any moral significance at all."[7] The popular, contemporary view is this:

- Homosexuality is a natural and normal variation in sexual expressiveness.

- Homosexuality is innate and cannot be changed, thus we should all accept it.
- Homosexual activity is harmless behavior between consenting adults.
- Homosexual marriage and parenting will not undermine nor weaken heterosexual family life.

We believe these assumptions about homosexuality have not resulted from better science or a more enlightened view of human rights, but have resulted from dramatic changes in religious and cultural values. First, society's norms on sexual behavior have been greatly altered to accept (or tolerate) almost any type of human sexual interaction. Nearly universal standards of sexual behavior (e.g., chastity, fidelity, and heterosexual monogamy) have fallen away with the slow but steady disintegration of religious belief and practice in America and Europe. The rise of secularism and pluralism has opened the door to almost any deviant sexual activity. Many people want the "freedom" to engage in any sexual behavior without restraint or condemnation. The new standard for human interaction is human rights without responsibility to societal well-being or to any greater good. Human rights are defined by individual preference, not by laws—human or divine.

Second, there are many gays and lesbians in positions of power and authority in government, the media, in academia, and in the religious community and they want social approval of their lifestyle choices.[8] They believe homosexual behavior must be normalized and accepted on equal grounds with heterosexual marriage. Their views hold sway for many Americans. Powerful forces are spreading the practices of sexual immorality and they wish to silence any and all opposition.[9] Wright and Cummings describe in detail how political correctness has created destructive trends in mental health including preventing research into the causes and consequences of homosexual behavior.[10]

Third, science and technology are the new gods of our culture. The magnificent achievements in physics, engineering, medicine, and computer science have ascended supreme. The computer chip has replaced the stone tablets of Moses as our guide to salvation. Thus, there is no God; there is no higher purpose than personal pleasure and fulfilling instinctual (primarily physical) urgencies. These then are three reasons why we believe attitudes have changed regarding homosexuality.

Our resistance to social acceptance of homosexuality is not really about judging private, consensual, adult behavior. That's not our primary concern. If, as adults, homosexuals kept their behavior private we would be much less worried, but there is an element within the homosexual community that seeks to tear down heterosexual marriage, sexually exploit youth, and force the homosexual agenda upon everyone.[11] Widespread recognition and legal sanction of homosexuality will redefine marriage.[12] It will weaken the traditional, heterosexual, two-parent family which is already reeling from the effects of divorce and out-of-wedlock births.[13] Widespread homosexuality further reduces the restrictions (and taboos) regulating all sexual behavior and so more children will suffer sexual abuses.[14] Charles Socarides, a psychiatrist who has treated many homosexuals, warns:

> The homosexual rights movement claims a freedom to alter that basic design [of marriage], to assert that all forms of sexual relations are equal and indistinguishable. *But this freedom, I submit... is a freedom that goes too far, because it undoes us.* It is a freedom that seeks to overturn not only the history of the human race, but to subvert its future as well. [It] dares to re-form the most basic institution of society, the nuclear family, an institution that is written in our natures and evolved over eons.[15]

What is to be Done?

Many parents believe that heterosexuality will manifest itself on its own, without teaching or reinforcement. Parents may believe there is no need to do anything. In most cases we agree. Heterosexuality is innate both spiritually and biologically. However, in today's promiscuous society youth are encouraged to question their sexual preference and to experiment with sexual behaviors. Even if one believes that heterosexuality is inherently natural, and will emerge on its own, teaching and encouragement may still be needed. Active involvement of parents may be necessary to guide some youth into heterosexuality. It is our hope that this book will add to the resources available to parents who support traditional gender identity and a heterosexual preference.

Bruce, in her insightful book *The New Thought Police, Inside the Left's Assault on Free Speech and Free Minds* makes a convincing case that today's sociopolitical climate does not allow people to criticize positions that are considered to be "politically correct." Bruce contends that "the fear of offending has effectively paralyzed any willingness we may once have had to engage society in debate over moral issues such as homosexuality."[16] Ms. Bruce is a feminist and a lesbian, yet she defends the right of others to speak their minds and participate in the debate over homosexuality.

Those who oppose the homosexual agenda should not be afraid to voice their opinions if it is done *without arrogance, anger, or condemnation towards any individual homosexual.* Refuse to be silenced by gay activists and elitist academics that preach political correctness and brook no dissent. Repudiate the label "homophobia," and refuse to be cowered by its use as a term of slander and derision. If you speak out be prepared to be criticized; gay activists will try to silence you by shaming and intimidation.[17]

Treating Unwanted Homosexual Attractions

For those who experience unwanted homosexual attraction, hope and healing is possible.[18] Many research studies and numerous personal accounts indicate that change is achievable, though difficult.[19] John Westcott, a former homosexual, now married, responded to those who claim that change is not possible: "Some people hate us because if we're living the truth [giving up homosexuality], then they're living a lie."[20] Howard, an ex-lesbian, makes this plea:

> There are many women who have tried to go straight and have failed. Perhaps their vision for change died, or they were influenced by the world, or felt overwhelmed by seemingly insurmountable difficulties. Whatever the reason, they found the task too daunting. We must not be surprised or discouraged when we hear of failure ... Just as we did not suddenly become lesbians, we will not suddenly become heterosexual. There is no quick fix method to healing. But healing is a reality ... The choice is yours. You can choose to remain in the bondage of lesbianism or you can leave it ... Change is possible.[21]

Another young woman described her struggle to overcome homosexual behavior in this way: "There was a time in my life when I believed there was no hope for me—no future—and that I would never come close to being [healed]... I wondered if I could ever be free of the bondage I was in."[22] She counseled with her pastor, prayed and fasted, read scriptures, and cleaned out her house of sexually suggestive music, videos, and books. She avoided people and places that would entice her back into homosexual activity. She then concluded, "My path has not been without struggles, but at last I have found the peace I craved for so many years ... I have emerged from the bondage that held me captive for so long."[23] Other stories of gays leaving homosexuality can be found at these websites: www.narth.com, www.gay-tostraight.org, www.peoplecanchange.com, and www.exodus.to (Exodus International).

In general, successful treatment of unwanted homosexuality is more likely to result from a combination of secular counseling and religious faith.[24] Fitzgibbons stated that the degree of emotional pain suffered by many homosexuals is so profound "that there is no mental health technique that can totally resolve this pain without a spiritual component."[25] He continues, "As a therapist I deal with the psychological. Yet I must admit there is little meaningful healing without the use of spirituality. If we combine spirituality and good psychotherapy as in the treatment of alcoholism we can expect resolution and healing for those who struggle with same-sex attraction."[26]

Some Final Thoughts

In closing, let us remind the reader that we have no ill-will toward those who engage in homosexual behavior or promote its social acceptance and the legality of same-sex marriage. But without doubt or apology, we believe that homosexual behavior is misdirected and will not bring the freedom and happiness that its participants and advocates promise. Individuals, both gay and straight, have been bedazzled and bullied into accepting homosexuality as normal and healthy, but it is not.[27]

Furthermore, we assert that homosexual behavior is inherently un-healthy and will lead to personal mental health problems and dysfunctional relationships. Many researchers report that gays and lesbians are more likely than heterosexuals to experience mental health problems such as depression, anxiety, thoughts of suicide, bulimia, substance abuse, and addictions.[28] Gays and their allies in academia, medicine, and the media claim these problems are *completely* the result of society's intolerance, bigotry, and narrow-mindedness.

We disagree. Homosexual behavior is intrinsically flawed and it is the behavior—and the rampant promiscuity and the instability of many homosexual relationships—that leads to a greater risk for mental (and physical) health problems, not society's negative attitudes, though this too may contribute. The social stigma of homosexuality is gradually but consistently fading away (in the US and throughout the western world), yet the increased risk of mental health problems for gays and lesbians has not appeared to decrease even in places like Denmark, Netherlands, and Sweden where there is overwhelming approval and support for homosexuality.[29]

Our goal in writing this book was (1) to provide insights into the roots and causes of homosexuality and (2) to provide information and practical advice to those who want to encourage heterosexuality and traditional marriage. We sought to dispel the myth that homosexuality is completely genetic and therefore unchangeable.[30] Biology may predispose an individual's temperament and personality and put a child at greater risk for developing homosexuality, but hereditary predisposition is a far cry from genetic predestination. Even the American Psychological Association (APA) in a recent statement has backed off their previous position that genetics determined homosexuality, and has declared:

> There is no consensus among scientists about the exact reasons that an individual develops a heterosexual, bisexual, gay or lesbian orientation. Although much research has examined the possible genetic, hormonal, developmental, social, and cultural influences on sexual orientation, no findings have emerged that permit scientists to conclude that sexual orientation is determined by any particular factor or factors.[31]

It is clear to us that homosexual behavior can best be understood from a broader perspective that includes spiritual, psychological, social, and biological influences. However, we still judge that environmental factors such as (a) dysfunctional parenting, (b) sexual abuse or sexual seduction, (c) early sexual experimentation, (d) pornography, (e) lack of moral education, and (f) misuse of moral agency are the major factors that combine in various ways to produce a homosexual outcome. Environmental trauma and moral agency are the main contributors to homosexuality.

In this book we have combined secular and scientific information with our personal religious beliefs. Many will claim out approach is scientifically flawed and religiously biased—and we admit this could be the case. We also recognize that our understanding of homosexuality is incomplete —we don't have all the answers. Yet we are confident that there are important truths in this book. Nevertheless, study these things out in your own mind. Consider the scientific evidence and the religious arguments. Integrate these two sources of information with your own values and insights. With a sincere desire, and by study and faith, a person can come to an understanding of God's divine plan for heterosexual families. If a parent receives an inner certainty of the veracity of heterosexuality, that individual will be better equipped to guide children into traditional male or female gender identity and into a heterosexual preference.

Robert Frost (1874-1963) penned the poem "The Road Not Taken". The final lines read: *"Two roads diverged in a wood, and I took the one less traveled by, and that made all the difference."* If children are chaste before marriage and then choose a heterosexual marriage, *this will make all the difference, too.* Traveling the virtuous road—the path of chastity and then heterosexuality—will propel youth into adulthood with peace, hope, and happiness. A Christian preacher wrote, many years ago, that *"Happiness is the object and design of our existence; and will be the end thereof, if we pursue the path that leads to; and this path is virtue."*[32]

AFTERWORD

The writing of this book has been a journey for us. It has taken a great deal of time and patience as we searched for the sources of truth from the best books, including both scientific treatises and the Holy Scriptures. We are braced for criticism from both the religious and scientific communities as we have reached a single conclusion: truth is discovered, not socially constructed. And, as noted by George Orwell, "In a time of universal deceit, telling the truth is a revolutionary act." Here are the truths that we have discovered.

The preeminence of the male-female relationship is a biological reality and a spiritual certainty. Gender, what it means to be male or female, is as much a characteristic of our spiritual selves as it is our social-biological selves. Gender differences are the basis for the family. Wholeness and health result from following the form and function designed by our creator. The heterosexual family is ordained of God. Thus, heterosexual unions not only serve our culture and society well but are protective for individuals, and particularly for children.

Mothers and fathers contribute in complementary ways to the healthy development of children. Two men, no matter how well-intentioned or well-meaning cannot be a mommy to a little girl. Neither can two women be a daddy to a little boy. The best interests of children are served by having a mother and father, each possessing different spiritual and biological strengths to care for them.

We concur and urge others to bring up their children in light and truth--but without criticism or disrespect for those who believe or act differently. By so doing children will grow up with "clean hands and pure hearts" and reap the rewards and blessings of heterosexual marriage and family life (The Bible, Psalms 24: 3-4).

APPENDIX A

For those wanting more information about understanding and overcoming homosexuality, a list of recommended books and on-line resources is provided.

1. *A Parent's Guide to Preventing Homosexuality*, by Joseph and Linda Nicolosi, Downers Grove, IL: InterVarsity Press, 2002.

2. *Homosexuality and the Politics of Truth*, by Jeffrey Satinover, Grands Rapids, MI, Baker Books, 1996.

3   *Dark obsession: the Tragedy and Threat of the Homosexual Lifestyle*, by Timothy J. Dailey, Nashville, TN: Broadman & Holman Publishers, 2003.

4. *Getting It Straight: What the Research Shows about Homosexuality*, by Peter Sprigg and Timothy Dailey, Washington, DC: The Family Research Council, 2004.

5. *Homosexuality: A Freedom Too Far*, by Charles Socarides, MD, Phoenix, AZ: Adam Margrave Books, 1995.

6. *The New Thought Police: Inside the Left's Assault on Free Speech and Free Minds*, by Tammy Bruce, Roseville, CA: Prima Publishing, 2001.

7. *Homosexuality and American Public Life*, by Christopher Wolfe (Editor), Dallas, TX: Spence Publishing, (1999).

8. *Growing Up Straight, What Every Family Should Know about Homosexuality*, by Dr. George Rekers, Chicago, IL: Moody Press, 1982.

9. *Coming out of homosexuality: New freedom for men and women*, by Bob Davies and Lori Rentzer, Westmont, IL: Intervarsity Press, 1994.

10. The Family Research Council, *<www.frc.org>*. Information on many traditional family topics is provided including homosexuality.

11. National Association for Research and Treatment of Homosexuality (NARTH) *<www.narth.com>*. This site was developed by Joseph Nicolosi and has many articles and resources.

Footnote References

Note: References have three parts: (1) The author's last name and first initial, (2) The name of the book or the title of the journal article, and (3) the publication information. If the source is a journal article, the journal name is followed by the volume number and then the page numbers. For example: The Family Journal, volume 15, pages 36-45 is written: *The Family Journal, 15,* 36-45.

FOREWORD

1. Maxwell, N. A. (1976). Some thoughts on the Gospel and the behavioral sciences. *Ensign*, July, pp. 70-74.

2. *The Bible*, 1st Corinthians chapter 1, verse 23.

3. We paraphrase from *The Bible*, Romans 12: 2.

4. *The Bible*, 1st Corinthians 2: 13-14.

5. *The Book of Mormon*, 2 Nephi 9:28.

6. C. S. Lewis, *Mere Christianity, 1980, p. 49.*

7. *The Book of Mormon*, Mormon 5: 16, also Ephesians 4:14.

8. *The Bible*, Ephesians 2: 12.

9. *The Bible*, 2nd Timothy 3:7.

10. *The Bible*, Matthew 7: 1.

11. *The Bible*, St. John 8: 1-11.

12. *The Bible*, Exodus 20: 1-17.

13. Alexander Pope (1688-1744), critic, satirist, and one of England's greatest poets, from *An Essay on Man: Epistle II, Stanza V, Lines 117-220.*

14. *The Bible*, Old Testament, Book of Isaiah, chapter 5 verse 20.

CHAPTER 1

1. Browning, D., Green, C., & Witte, J. (2006). *Sex, marriage, and family in world religions.* New York, NY: Columbia University Press.

2. Murray, S. O., & Roscoe, W. (1997). *Islamic homosexualities*. NY: New York University Press. Swidler, A. (1993). *Homosexuality and world religions*. Valley Forge, PA: Trinity Press.

3. Giele, J. Z. (2007). Decline of the family: Conservative, liberal, and feminist views. In A. Skolnick, & J. Skolnick (Eds.), *Family in Transition* 14th Edition, pages 76–95. Strong, B, Sayad, B., & Yarber, W. (2006). *Human sexuality: diversity in contemporary America*. Boston, MA: McGraw-Hill.

4. Bennett, W. J. (2001). *The broken hearth: reversing the moral collapse of the American family*. New York, NY: Doubleday.

5. Bennett, W. J. (2003). A man and a woman are needed for the honorable estate. In M. Coleman and L. Ganong (Eds.), *Points & counterpoints, controversial relationship and family issues in the 21st century*. Los Angles, CA: Roxbury Publishing. Cohen, R. (2001). *Coming out straight: Understanding and healing homosexuality*. Winchester, VA: Oakhill Press.

6. Schwartz, M., & Scott, B. M. (2007). *Marriages and families Fifth edition*. Upper Saddle River, NJ: Pearson/Prentice Hall. Welch, K. J. (2007). *Family life now: A conversation about marriages, families, and relationships*. Boston: Pearson Education.

7. Perry, J. & Perry R. (2006). *Contemporary society: An introduction to social science*. Boston, MA: Allyn and Bacon.

8. Buxton, A. P. (2006). When a spouse comes out: Impact on the heterosexual partner. *Sexual Addiction & Compulsivity, 13,* 317–332. Yarhouse, M. & Nowacki, S. (2007). The many meanings of marriage: divergent perspectives seeking common ground. *The Family Journal, 15,* 36–45.

9. Bogaert, A. F. (2007). Extreme right-handedness, older brothers, and sexual orientation in men. *Neuropsychology, 21,* 141–148. Garnets, L., & Kimmel, D. C. (1993). Lesbian and gay male dimensions in the psychological study of human diversity. In L. Garnets and D. Kimmer (Eds.), *Psychological perspectives on lesbian and gay male experiences, pp. 1-51.* New York, NY: Columbia University Press.
Kurdek, L. (2004). Gay men and lesbians: The family context. In M. Coleman and L. Ganong (Eds.), *Handbook of contemporary families: Considering the past contemplating the future, pp. 96–115.* Thousand Oaks, CA: Sage.

10. Greenberg, J., Bruess, C., & Haffner, D. (2002). *Exploring the dimensions of human sexuality*. Boston, MA: Jones and Bartlett Publishers.

11. American Psychological Association. (1975). Minutes of the Council of Representatives. *American Psychologist, 30,* 633. Bieschke, K., Perez, R., DeBord, K. (2007). *Handbook of counseling and psychotherapy with lesbian, gay, bisexual, and transgender clients (2nd Edition)*. Washington, DC: American Psychological Association. Satinover, J. (1996). *Homosexuality and the politics of truth*. Grand Rapids, MI: Baker Books. Stacey, J. (2007. Gay and lesbian families:

Queer like us. In A. Skolnick, & J. Skolnick (Eds.), *Family in Transition* 14th Edition, pp. 448–469. Boston, MA: Allyn & Bacon.

12. Boswell, J. (1980). *Christianity, social tolerance, and homosexuality.* Chicago, IL: University of Chicago Press. Helminiak, D. A. (1997). *The Bible on homosexuality: Ethically neutral.* In J. Corvino (Ed.), *Same sex: Debating the ethics, science, and culture of homosexuality.* Lanham, MD: Rowman & Littlefield Publishers, Inc. 81–103. Leckie, W., & Stopfel, B. (1997). *Courage to love: a gay priest stands up for his beliefs. New York, NY: Doubleday.* Marciano, T. D. (1985). Homosexual marriage and parenthood should be allowed. In H. Feldman and M. Feldman (Eds.), *Current controversies in marriage and family, pp. 293–302.* Beverly Hills, CA: Sage Publications.

13. White, M. (1994). *Stranger at the gate: to be gay and Christian in America.* New York, NY: Simon & Schuster. Yip, A. K. (1997). *Gay male Christian couples: Life stories.* Westport, CT: Praeger.

14. Nicolosi, J., & Nicolosi, L. A. (2002). *A parent's guide to preventing homosexuality.* Downers Grove, IL: InterVarsity Press.

15. Loftus, J. (2001). America's liberalization in attitudes toward homosexuality, 1973–1998. *American Sociological Review, 66,* 762–782. Kaiser Family Foundation. (2001). Inside-out: A report on the experiences of lesbians, gays, and bisexuals in American and the public's view of issues and politics related to sexual orientation. Available online at: www.kff.org. Yang, A. (1997). Attitudes toward homosexuality. *Public Opinion Quarterly, 6,* 477–507.

16. Sullivan, M. (2003). *Sexual minorities: discrimination, challenges and development in America.* New York, Haworth Press.

17. Berrill, K. T. (1992). Anti-gay violence and victimization in the United States: An overview. In G. M. Herek, G. M. (1989). Hate crimes against lesbians and gay men: Issues for research and policy. *American Psychologist, 44,* 948–955. Wolfe, C. (1999). Preface. In C. Wolfe (Ed.), Homosexuality and American public life, pp. ix-xiv. Dallas, TX: Spence Publishing.

18. Dailey, T. J. (2003). *Dark obsession: the tragedy and threat of the homosexual lifestyle.* Nashville, TN: Broadman & Holman Publishers.

19. Eisenberg, M., & Resnick, M. (2006). Suicidality among gay lesbian, and bisexual youth: There role of protective factors. *Journal of Adolescent Health, 39,* 662–668.

20. Bennett, W. J. (2003). A man and a woman are needed for the honorable estate. In M. Coleman and L. Ganong (Eds.), *Points & counterpoints, controversial relationship and family issues in the 21st century, p. 83.* Los Angles, CA: Roxbury Publishing.

21. Oaks, Dallin H. "Our Strengths Can Become Our Downfall," Ensign, Oct. 1994, p. 11.

22. Oaks, Dallin H. "Our Strengths Can Become Our Downfall," Ensign, Oct. 1994, p. 12.

23. Packer, Boyd K. "Covenants." *The Ensign*. Nov. 1990, p. 84.

24. LeVay, S. (2000). Sexual Orientation: The science and its social impact, 12. Retrieved April 3, 2001 from http://members.aol.com/_ht_a/slevay/page12. htm.

25. Hamer, D. H. & Copeland, P. (1994). *The Science of Desire*. New York: Simon & Schuster, p. 214.

CHAPTER 2

1. Burr, W. R. (1995). Using theories in family science. In R. D. Day (Ed.), *Research and theory in family science, pp. 73–89*. Pacific Grove, CA: Brooks/Cole Publishing.

2. Smith, H. (2001). *Why religion matters*. San Francisco, CA: Harper Collins.

3. Thomas, D., & Rogharr, H. (1990). Post positivist theorizing: The case of religion and the family. In J. Sprey (Ed.), *Fashioning family theory: new approaches*. Newbury Park, CA: Sage.

4. Greenberg, S. (2005). *Wrestling with God and men: Homosexuality in the Jewish tradition*. Madison, WI: University of Wisconsin Press. Via, D. O., & Gagnon, R. A. (2003). *Homosexuality and the Bible: Two views*. Minneapolis, MN: Augsburg Fortress Publishers. White, J. R., & Niell, J. (2002). *Same sex controversy*. Minneapolis, MN: Bethany House Publishers.

5. Hasbany. R. (1990). *Homosexuality and religion*. Binghamton, NY: Haworth Press. Jakobsen, J. R. & Pellegrini, A. (2004). *Love the sin: Sexual regulation and the limits of religious tolerance*. Boston, MA: Beacon Press. Long, R. E. (2004). *Men, homosexuality, and the Gods*. Binghamton, NY: Haworth Press. McNeil, J. J. (1993). *The church and the homosexual*. Boston, MA: Beacon Press. Moon, D. (2004). *God, sex, and politics: homosexuality and everyday theologies*. Chicago, IL: University of Chicago Press. White, M. (1994). *Stranger at the gate: to be gay and Christian in America*. New York, NY: Simon & Schuster.

6. Dailey, T. J. (2003). *Dark obsession: the tragedy and threat of the homosexual lifestyle*. Nashville, TN: Broadman & Holman Publishers.

7. Smith, H. (2001). *Why religion matters*. San Francisco, CA: Harper Collins.

8. Howard, J. (2001). *Out of Egypt: One woman's journey out of lesbianism*. Grand Rapids, MI: Kregel Publications.

9. Durand, V. M., & Barlow, D. H. (2003). *Essentials of abnormal psychology*. Pacific Grove, CA: Wadsworth Publishing.

10. Bennett, W. J. (2001). *The broken hearth: reversing the moral collapse of the American family*. New York, NY: Doubleday. Knight, R. H. (1997). How

domestic partnerships and gay marriage threaten the family. In J. Corvino (Ed.), *Same sex. Debating the ethics, science, and culture of homosexuality, pp. 289–303*. Lanham, MD: Rowman & Littlefield Publishers, Inc. Wolfe, C. (1999). Preface. In C. Wolfe (Ed.), *Homosexuality and American public life*, pp. ix-xiv. Dallas, TX: Spence Publishing.

11. Balcom, D. A. (1998). Absent fathers: effects on abandoned sons. *The Journal of Men's Studies*, 6, 283–291. Byrd, A.D. & Byrd, K.M. (2007). Dual-Gender parenting: a social science perspective for optimal child rearing in Family Law, In Lynn D. Wardle and Camille Williams (Eds.), *Balancing Interests and Pursuing Priorities*, pp. 382–390. Buffalo, New York: William S. Hein. Byrd, A.D. & Cox, S.E. (2007). Strict scrutiny of prospective adoptive parents: what children really need. *In* A. Scott Loveless and Thomas B. Holman (Eds.), *The Family In The New Millennium*, pp. 204–219. Westpoint, Connecticut: Praeger,. Coley, R. L. (1998). Children's socialization experiences and functioning in single-mother households: The importance of fathers and other men. *Child Development*, 69, 219–230. Halle, T., Moore, K., Greene, A., & LeMenestrel, S. M. (1998). What policy makers need to know about fathers. *Journal of the American Public Human Services Association*, 56 (3), 21–32. Hetherington, M., & Kelly, J. (2002). *For better or for worse: Divorce reconsidered*. New York, NY: W. W. Norton. Wallenstein, J., Blakeslee, S., & Lewis, J. (2001). *The unexpected legacy of divorce: The 25 year landmark study*. New York, NY: Hyperion Press. Whitehead, B. D. (1993). Dan Quale was right. *Atlantic Monthly, 271*, 4, 47–85.

12. Levine, J. (2002). *Harmful to minors: The perils of protecting our children from sex*. Minneapolis, MN: University of Minnesota Press.

13. Constantine, L. L. (1981). The effects of early sexual experiences: A review and synthesis of research. In L. L. Constantine and F. M. Martinson (Eds.), *Children and sex: New findings, new perspectives, pp. 217–245*. Boston, MA: Little, Brown and Company. Graupner, H. (1999). Love versus abuse: Crossgenerational sexual relations of minors: A gay rights issues. *Journal of Homosexuality, 37* (4), 23–56. Li, C. K. (1990). The main thing is being wanted: Some case studies on adult sexual experiences with children. *Journal of Homosexuality*, 20, 129–143. Rind, B., Bauserman, R., & Tromovitch, P. (1998). A meta-analytic examination of assumed properties of child sexual abuse using college samples. *Psychological Bulletin*, 124, 22–53.

14. Constantine, L. L. (1981). The effects of early sexual experiences: A review and synthesis of research. In L. L. Constantine and F. M. Martinson (Eds.), *Children and sex: New findings, new perspectives, pp. 217–245*. Boston, MA: Little, Brown and Company. Thorstad, D. (1991). Man/boy love and the American gay movement. *Journal of Homosexuality, 20* (1/2), 251–272.

15. Moser, C. & Kleinplatz, P.J. (2003). "DSM-IV-TR and the Paraphilias: An Argument for Removal, "paper presented at the American Psychiatric Association annual conference, San Francisco, California, May 19.

16. Green, R. (2002). Is pedophilia a mental disorder? *Archives of Sexual Behavior*, 31, 6, 467–471. Schmidt, G. (2002) The Dilemma of the Male Pedophile. *Archives of Sexual Behavior*, 31, 473–477.

17. Baldwin, S. (2001/2002). Child molestation and the homosexual movement. *Regent University Law Review*, 14(2), 267–282.

18. Schmidt, T. (1995). *Straight and narrow?, p. 60.* Downer Grove, IL: InterVarsity Press.

19. Constantine, L. L. (1981). The sexual rights of children: Implications of a radical perspective. In L. L. Constantine and F. M. Martinson (Eds.), *Children and sex: New findings, new perspectives, p. 262.* Boston, MA: Little, Brown and Company.

20. Constantine, L. L. (1981). The sexual rights of children: Implications of a radical perspective. In L. L. Constantine and F. M. Martinson (Eds.), *Children and sex: New findings, new perspectives, p. 258.* Boston, MA: Little, Brown and Company.

21. Constantine, L. L. (1981). The sexual rights of children: Implications of a radical perspective. In L. L. Constantine and F. M. Martinson (Eds.), *Children and sex: New findings, new perspectives, p. 259.* Boston, MA: Little, Brown and Company.

22. Jones, G. P. (1991). The study of intergenerational intimacy in North Americans: Beyond politics and pedophilia. *Journal of Homosexuality, 20* (1/2), 275–291.

23. Baldwin, S. (2001/2002). Child molestation and the homosexual movement. *Regent University Law Review*, 14 (2), 270.

24. Dailey, T. J. (2003). *Dark obsession: the tragedy and threat of the homosexual lifestyle.* Nashville, TN: Broadman & Holman Publishers.

25. Dailey, T. J. (2003). *Dark obsession: the tragedy and threat of the homosexual lifestyle.* Nashville, TN: Broadman & Holman Publishers.

26. Jones, G. P. (1991). The study of intergenerational intimacy in North Americans: Beyond politics and pedophilia. *Journal of Homosexuality, 20* (1/2), 275–291. Sandfort, T., Brongersma, E., & van Naerssen, A. (1991). Man-boy relationships: Different concepts for a diversity of phenomena. *Journal of Homosexuality, 20* (1/2), 5–12. Rind, B., Bauserman, R., & Tromovitch, P. (1998). A meta-analytic examination of assumed properties of child sexual abuse using college samples. *Psychological Bulletin, 124*, 22–53.

27. Rind, B., Bauserman, R., & Tromovitch, P. (1998). A meta-analytic examination of assumed properties of child sexual abuse using college samples. *Psychological Bulletin, 124,* 22-53.

28. Brongersma, E. (1990). Boy-lovers and their influence on boys: distorted research and anecdotal observations. *Journal of Homosexuality, 20* (1/2), 162-67.

29. Jones, G. P. (1991). The study of intergenerational intimacy in North Americans: Beyond politics and pedophilia. *Journal of Homosexuality, 20* (1/2), 273-280.

30. Baldwin, S. (2001/2002). Child molestation and the homosexual movement. *Regent University Law Review,* 14(2), 267–282.

31. Holloway, C. (2003). *From playboy to pedophilia: how adult sexual liberation leads to children's sexual exploitation.* Paragraph 17. Retrieved from the web on 13 April, 2003, at <www. frc.org /get/wto2gl.cfm>.

32. Ball, C. A. (2003). *The morality of gay rights: An exploration in political philosophy.* New York, NY: Routledge. Haidt, J., & Hersh, M. A. (2001). Sexual morality: The cultures and emotions of conservatives and liberals. *Journal of Applied Social Psychology,* 31, 191–221.

33. Haidt, J., & Hersh, M. A. (2001). Sexual morality: The cultures and emotions of conservatives and liberals. *Journal of Applied Social Psychology,* 31, 191–221.

34. King, B. M. (2004). *Human sexuality today.* Upper Saddle River, NJ: Prentice Hall.

35. Jones, S. L., & Yarhouse, M. A. (2007). Ex-gays: a longitudinal study of religiously mediate change in sexual orientation. Downers Grove, IL: InterVarsity Press.

36. Jones, S. L., & Yarhouse, M. A. (2007). Ex-gays: a longitudinal study of religiously mediate change in sexual orientation. Downers Grove, IL: InterVarsity Press.

37. Roesler, T., & Deishner, R. W. (1972). Youthful male homosexuality: Homosexual experiences and the process of developing homosexual identity in males age 16 to 22 years. *Journal of the American Medical Association,* 219, 1021-1031.

38. Murray, S. O. (2000). *Homosexualities.* Chicago, IL: University of Chicago Press. Golden, C. (1994). Our politics, our choices: The feminist movement and sexual orientation . In B. Greene and G. Herek (Eds.), *Lesbian and gay psychology: Theory, research and clinical applications, pp. 54–70.* Thousand Oaks, CA: Sage Publications.

39. Medinger, A. (2000). *Growth into manhood*. Colorado Spring, CO: Water-Brook Press. Oaks, D. H. (1995). Same-gender attraction. *The Ensign*, October, pp. 7–14.

40. Medinger, A. (2000). *Growth into manhood*. Colorado Spring, CO: Water-Brook Press. p. 184.

41. Oaks, D. H. (1995). Same-gender attraction. *The Ensign*, October, p. 9.

42. Black, D. (2000). Demographics of the gay and lesbian population in the United States: Evidence from available systematic data sources. *Demography*, *37*, 150–162. Gonsiorek, J., & Weinrich, J. D. (1991). The definition and scope of sexual orientation. In J. Gonsiorek and J. Weinrich (Eds.), *Homosexuality: Research implications for public policy, pp. 1–12*. Newbury Park, CA: Sage Publications. Janus, S., & Janus, C. (1993). *The Janus report on sexual behavior*. New York, NY: John Wiley & Sons. King, B. M. (2004). *Human sexuality today*. Upper Saddle River, NJ: Prentice Hall. Laumann, E., Gagnon, J., Michael, R., Michaels, S., & Kolata, G. (1995). *Sex in America: A definitive survey*. Boston: Little, Brown. Michaels, S. (1996). The prevalence of homosexuality in the United States. In R. P. Cabaj and T. S. Stein (Eds.), *Textbook of homosexuality and mental health, pp. 44–64*. Washington, DC: American Psychiatric Press.

43. Allen, D. J., & Oleson, T. (1999). Shame and internalized homophobia in gay men. *Journal of Homosexuality, 37*, 33–43. Herek, G. M. (1996). Heterosexism and homophobia. In R. P. Cabaj and T. S. Stein (Eds.), *Textbook of homosexuality and mental health, pp. 101–113*. Washington, DC: American Psychiatric Press.

44. Greenberg, J., Bruess, C., & Haffner, D. (2002). *Exploring the dimensions of human sexuality*. Boston, MA: Jones and Bartlett Publishers.

45. O'Donohue, W., & Caselles, C. E. (1993). Homophobia: conceptual, definitional and value issues. *Journal of Psychopathology and Behavioral Assessment, 15*, 177–195.

46. Durand, V. M., & Barlow, D. H. (2003). *Essentials of abnormal psychology*. Pacific Grove, CA: Wadsworth Publishing.

47. O'Donohue, W., & Caselles, C. E. (1993). Homophobia: conceptual, definitional and value issues. *Journal of Psychopathology and Behavioral Assessment, 15*, 190.

48. Herek, G. M. (1996). Heterosexism and homophobia. In R. P. Cabaj and T. S. Stein (Eds.),*Textbook of homosexuality and mental health*, p. 101. Washington, DC: American Psychiatric Press.

49. Herek, G. M. (1996). Heterosexism and homophobia. In R. P. Cabaj and T. S. Stein (Eds.),*Textbook of homosexuality and mental health,* pp. 101–113. Washington, DC: American Psychiatric Press,

50. Szuchman, L.T., & Muscarella, F. (2000). *Psychological perspectives on human sexuality*. New York: John Wiley & Sons.

51. Bradley, S. J., & Zucker, K. J. (1997). Gender identity disorder: A review of the past 10 years. *Journal of the American Academy of Child and Adolescent Psychiatry*, 36, 872–880.

52. Halderman, D. C. (1994). The practice and ethics of sexual orientation conversion therapy. *Journal of Consulting and Clinical Psychology, 62*, 221-232.

53. Coleman, E. (1990). Toward a synthetic understanding of sexual orientation. In D. McWhirter, S. Sanders and J. Reinisch, *Homosexuality/Heterosexuality, concepts of sexual orientation, pp. 267–277.* New York, NY: Oxford University Press. Klein, F. (1990). The need to view sexual orientation as a multivariable dynamic process. In D. McWhirter, S. Sanders and J. Reinisch (Eds.), *Homosexuality/ Heterosexuality, concepts of sexual orientation, pp. 277–282.* New York, NY: Oxford University Press.

54. Bradley, S. J., & Zucker, K. J. (1997). Gender identity disorder: A review of the past 10 years. *Journal of the American Academy of Child and Adolescent Psychiatry*, 36, 872–880.

55. Byer, C. O., Shriver, S., Shainberg, W., & Galliano, G. (2001). *Dimensions of human sexuality*. Boston, MA: McGraw Hill.

56. Miracle, T. S., Miracle A. W., & Baumeister, R. F. (2003). *Human sexuality meeting your basic needs*. Upper Saddle River, NJ: Prentice Hall.

57. Durand, V. M., & Barlow, D. H. (2003). *Essentials of abnormal psychology*. Pacific Grove, CA: Wadsworth Publishing.

CHAPTER 3

1. Green, M., & Piel, J. (2002). *Theories of human development: A comparative approach*. Boston, MA: Allyn and Bacon.

2. White, J., & Klein, D. (2002). *Family theories (2nd editions)*. Thousand Oaks, CA: Sage.

3. Lutzker, J. (1998). *Handbook of child abuse research and treatment.*, NY: Plenum Press, 1998.

4. Eisenberg, N., & Fabes, R. (1998). Prosocial development. In W. Damon and N. Eisenberg (Eds.), *Handbook of child psychology*, pp. 701–778.

5. Bailey, J. M. (1995). Biological perspectives on sexual orientation. In A. R. D'Augelli and C. J. Patterson (Eds.), *Lesbian, gay and bisexual identities over the lifespan*. NY: Oxford University Press. 102–135. Isay, R. A. (1997). *Becoming gay: The journey of self-acceptance*. New York, NY: Holt and Company.

6. Ellis, L., & Ames, M. A. (1987). Neurohormonal functioning and sexual orientation: A theory of homosexuality-heterosexuality. *Psychological Bulletin,*

101, 223–250. Kelly, S. J., Ostrowski, N. L, & Wilson, M. A. (1999). Gender differences in brain and behavior: Hormonal and neural bases. *Pharmacology Biochemistry & Behavior, 64*, 655–664.

7. Nicolosi, J. (1991). *Reparative therapy of male homosexuality: A new clinical approach.* Northvale, NJ: Jason Aronson, Inc. Socarides, C. (1995). *Homosexuality: A freedom too far.* Phoenix, AZ: Adam Margrave.

8. Tomeo, E., Templer, D. I., Anderson, S., & Kotler, D. (2001) Comparative data of childhood and adolescence molestation in heterosexual and homosexual persons. *Archives of Sexual Behavior, 30*, 535–541.

9. Dahir, M. (2001). Why are we gay? *The Advocate*, July 17, pp. 30–42. Silverstein, C. (1991). Psychological and medical treatments of homosexuality. In J. Gonsiorek and J. Weinrich (Eds.), *Homosexuality: Research implications for public policy, pp. 101–114.* Newbury Park, CA: Sage Publications.

10. Bailey, J. M. (1995). Biological perspectives on sexual orientation. In A. R. D'Augelli and C. J. Patterson (Eds.), *Lesbian, gay and bisexual identities over the lifespan, pp.*102–135. NY: Oxford University Press.

11. LeVay, S. (1991). A difference in hypothalamic structure between heterosexual and homosexual men. *Science*, 253, 1034–1037. Swaab, D. F., Gooren, L. J., & Hofman, M. A. (1992). The human hypothalamus in relation to gender and sexual orientation. *Progress in Brain Research*, 93, 205–219.

12. Kaplan, H. S., & Owett, T. (1993). The female androgen deficiency syndrome. *Journal of Sex & Martial Therapy, 19,* 3–24. Meyer-Bahlburg, H., Ehrhardt, A. A., Rosen, L. R., Gruen, R. S., Veridiano, N. P., Vann, F. H., & Newwalder, H. F. (1995). Prenatal estrogens and the development of homosexual orientations. *Developmental Psychology*, 31, 12–21.

13. Hamer, D. H., Hu, S., Magnuson, V. L., Hu, N., & Pattatucci, A. (1993). A linkage between DNA markers on the X chromosome and male sexual orientations. *Science*, 261, 321–327.

14. Weinrich, J. D. (1995). Biological research on sexual orientation: A critique of the critics. *Journal of Homosexuality, 28*, 197–213.

15. Byne, W. (1996). Biology and homosexuality: Implication fo neuroendocrinological and neuroanatomical studies. In R. P. Cabaj and T. S. Stein (Eds.), *Textbook of homosexuality and mental health, pp. 123-* 131. Washington, DC: American Psychiatric Press.

16. Byne, W. (1996). Biology and homosexuality: Implication fo neuroendocrinological and neuroanatomical studies. In R. P. Cabaj and T. S. Stein (Eds.), *Textbook of homosexuality and mental health,* p. 131. Washington, DC: American Psychiatric Press.

17. Carey, G. (2003). *Human genetics for the social sciences.* Thousand Oaks, CA: Sage.

18. Carey, G. (2003). *Human genetics for the social sciences.* Thousand Oaks, CA: Sage.

19. Bazzett, T. J. (2008). *An introduction to behavioral genetics.* Sunderland, MA: Sinauer Associates.

20. Kolb, B., & Whishaw, I. Q. (2004). *An introduction to brain and behavior.* New York: Worth

21. Plomin, R., DeFries, J., & McClearn, G. (1980). *Behavioral genetics: a primer.* San Francisco, CA: W. H. Freeman.

22. Parens, E., Chapman, A, & Press, N. (2006). *Wrestling with behavioral genetics: science, ethics, and public conversation.* Baltimore, MD: Johns Hopkins University Press. Rutter, M. (2006). *Genes and behavior nature-nurture interplay explained.* Ames, IO: Blackwell Publishing.

23. Collins, F. S. (2006). *The language of god, a scientist presents evidence for belief,* pp. 263, 260. New York: Free Press.

24. Lewontin, R. C. (1991). *Biology as ideology: The doctrine of DNA, p. 251.* New York: Harper Collins.

25. Stein, E. (1999). *The mismeasure of desire: The science, theory, and ethics of sexual orientation.* New York, NY: Oxford University Press.

26. Baker, C. (2004). *Behavioral genetics: An introduction to how genes and environments interact throughout development to shape differences in mood, personality, and intelligence, pp.* 17–18. New York: The American Association for the Advancement of Science and the Hastings Center. Entire book available free online at: http://www.aaas.org/spp/bgenes/publications.shtml.

27. Hubbard, R., & Wald, E. (1999). *Exploding the gene myth,* p. 44. Boston, MA: Beacon Press.

28. Rutter, M. (2006). *Genes and behavior nature-nurture interplay explained.* Ames, IO: Blackwell Publishing.

29. Hubbard, R., & Wald, E. (1999). *Exploding the gene myth.* Boston, MA: Beacon Press.

30. Plomin, R., DeFries, J., & McClearn, G. (1980). *Behavioral genetics: a primer, p. 259.* San Francisco, CA: W. H. Freeman.

31. Moore, A. (2007). Gay-rights leader quits homosexuality. Posted on July 3, 2007 and available on-line at: http://www.worldnetdaily.com.

32. Moore, A. (2007). Gay-rights leader quits homosexuality, pp. 3–5. Posted on July 3, 2007 and available on-line at: http://www.worldnetdaily.com.

33. Odent, M. (2005). Genesis of sexual orientation: From Plato to Dorner. *Journal of Prenatal & Perinatal Psychology & Health, 20* (2), 49–47.

34. Johnson, M. D. (2007). *Human biology: Concepts and current issues.* Upper Saddle River, NJ: Benjamin Cummings/Pearson.

35. Byne, W. (2007). Biology and sexual minority status. In I. Meyer and M. Northridge (Eds.), *The health of sexual minorities: Public health perspectives on lesbian, gay, bisexual, and transgender populations,* pp. 65-90. New York: Springer. LeVay, S. (1991). A difference in hypothalamic structure between heterosexual and homosexual men. *Science, 253,* 1034–1037.

36. Veridiano, N. P., Vann, F., & Neuwalder, H. (1995). Prenatal estrogens and the development of homosexual orientation. *Developmental Psychology, 31,* 1, 12-21.

37. Kaplan, H. S., & Owett, T. (1993). The female androgen deficiency syndrome. *Journal of Sex & Martial Therapy, 19,* 3–24. Meyer-Bahlburg, H., Ehrhardt, A. A., Rosen, L. R., Gruen, R. S., Veridiano, N. P., Vann, F. H., & Newwalder, H. F. (1995). Prenatal estrogens and the development of homosexual orientations. *Developmental Psychology,* 31, 12–21.

38. Gooren, L. (2006). The biology of human psychosexual differentiation. *Hormones and Behavior, 50,* 589-601.

39. Banks, A., & Gartrell, N. K. (1995). Hormones and sexual orientations: A questionable link. *Journal of Homosexuality, 28,* 263-267.

40. Banks, A., & Gartrell, N. K. (1995). Hormones and sexual orientations: A questionable link. *Journal of Homosexuality, 28,* 248-255.

41. Wilson, G. & Rahman, Q. (2005). *Born gay: the psychobiology of sex orientation.* London: Peter Owen.

42. Habr-Alencar, S., Dias, R., Teodorov, E., & Bernardi, M. (2006). The effect of hetero- and homosexual experience and long-term treatment with fluoxetine on homosexual behavior in male rats. *Psychopharmacology, 189,* 269-275.

43. Gooren, L. (2006). The biology of human psychosexual differentiation. *Hormones and Behavior, 50,* 591-1009.

44. Byne, W. (2007). Biology and sexual minority status. In I. Meyer and M. Northridge (Eds.), *The health of sexual minorities: Public health perspectives on lesbian, gay, bisexual, and transgender populations,* pp. 65-90. New York: Springer.

45. Bancroft, J. (1990). Commentary: Biological contributions to sexual orientation. In D. McWhirter, S. A. Sanders, and J. M. Reinisch (Eds.). *Homosexuality heterosexuality concepts of sexual orientation, p. 109.* New York, NY: Oxford University Press.

46. Bozett, F. W. (1987). *Gay and lesbian parents.* New York, NY: Praeger. Bigner, J. J., & Bozett, F. W. (1989). Parenting by gay fathers. *Marriage and Family Review,* 14, 155–175. Golombok, S., Spence, A., & Rutter, M. (1983). Children in lesbian and single parent households: Psychosexual and psychiatric ap-

praisal. *Journal of Child Psychology and Psychiatry*, 24, 551–572. Gottman, J. S. (1990). Children of gay and lesbian parents. *Marriage and Family Review*, 14, 177–196. Patterson, C. J. (1992). Children of lesbian and gay parents. *Child Development*, 63, 1025–1042.

47. Fitzgerald, B. (1999). Children of lesbian and gay parents: A review of the literature. *Marriage & Family Review, 29*, 57–75.

48. Lerner, R., & Nagai, A. (2002). Marriage policy and the methodology of research on homosexual parenting. In A. J. Hawkins, L. Wardle, and D. Collidge (Eds.), *Revitalizing the institution of marriage for the twenty-first century: an agenda for strengthening marriage, pp. 155–166.* Westport, CT: Praeger. Rekers, G., & Kilgus, M. (2001/2002). Studies of homosexual parenting: A critical review. *Regent University Law Review, 14* (2), 343–382.

49. Barmrind, D. (1995). Commentary on sexual orientation: Research and social policy implications. *Developmental Psychology, 31*, 130–136. Golombok, S., & Tasker, F. (1996). Do parents influence the sexual orientation of their children? *Developmental Psychology, 32*, 1–11.

50. Byne W., & Parsons, B. (1993). Human sexual orientation: The biological theories reappraised. *Archives of General Psychiatry*, 50, 237.

51. Szuchman, L.T., & Muscarella, F. (2000). *Psychological perspectives on human sexuality.* New York: John Wiley & Sons. 212.

52. Parker, D. A., & DeCecco, J. P. (1995). Sexual expression: A global perspective. *Journal of Homosexuality, 28*, 427-438.

53. Friedman, R. C. & Downey, J.I. (1994). Homosexuality. *New England Journal of Medicine, 331*, 923-939.

54. Friedman, R.C., & Downey, J.I., (2002) Sexual orientation and psychoanalysis: sexual science and clinical practice, p. 39. New York: Columbia University Press.

55. Dreifus, C. (2001, January 2). "Exploring what makes us male and female," *New York Times*, Science Section.

56. Paglia, C. (1994). *Vamps and tramps,* p71. New York: Vintage Books.

57. Valenstein, E. S. (1998). *Blaming the brain: The truth about drugs and mental health.* New York, NY: The Free Press. 140–141, 224.

58. Bieber, I. (1976). A discussion of homosexuality: The ethical challenge. *Journal of Consulting and Clinical Psychology*, 44, 163–166.

59. Friedman, R. C. (1988). *Male homosexuality: A contemporary psychoanalytic perspective.* New Haven, CT: Yale University Press.

60. Fitzgibbons, R. (1999). The origins and therapy of homosexual attraction disorder. In C. Wolfe (Ed.), *Homosexuality and American public life*, pp. 85–97. Dallas, TX: Spence. Zucker, K. J., & Bradley, S. J. (1995). *Gender identity*

disorder and psychosexual problems in children and adolescents., NY: Guilford Press.

61. Nicolosi, J. (1991). *Reparative therapy of male homosexuality: A new clinical approach.* Northvale, NJ: Jason Aronson, Inc.

62. Davies, B., & Rentzer, L. (1994). *Coming out of homosexuality: New freedom for men and women.* Westmont, IL: InterVarsity Press.

63. Zucker, K. J., & Bradley, S. J. (1995). *Gender identity disorder and psychosexual problems in children and adolescents.* NY: Guilford Press.

64. Zucker, K. J., & Bradley, S. J. (1995). *Gender identity disorder and psychosexual problems in children and adolescents.* NY: Guilford Press.

65. Wolff, C. (1971). *Love between women.* NY: Harper & Row.

66. Loney, J. (1973). Family dynamics in homosexual women. *Archives of Sexual Behavior, 2,* 348.

67. Loney, J. (1973). Family dynamics in homosexual women. *Archives of Sexual Behavior, 2,* 349.

68. Zucker, K. J., & Bradley, S. J. (1995). *Gender identity disorder and psychosexual problems in children and adolescents.* New York, NY: Guilford Press.

69. Zucker, K. J., & Bradley, S. J. (1995). *Gender identity disorder and psychosexual problems in children and adolescents.* New York, NY: Guilford Press.

70. Zucker, K. J., & Bradley, S. J. (1995). *Gender identity disorder and psychosexual problems in children and adolescents.* New York, NY: Guilford Press.

71. Zucker, K. J., & Bradley, S. J. (1995). *Gender identity disorder and psychosexual problems in children and adolescents.* New York, NY: Guilford Press.

72. Rosen, D. H. (1974). *Lesbianish: A study of female homosexuality.* Springfield, IL: C. C. Thomas Publishing. Socarides, C. (1995). *Homosexuality: A freedom too far.* Phoenix, AZ: Adam Margrave.

73. Bandura, A. (1977). *Social Learning Theory.* Englewood Cliffs, N.J: Prentice-Hall. Bandura, A., & Walters, R. H. (1963). *Social learning and personality development.* New York, NY: Holt, Rinehart & Winston.

74. Bandura, A. (1986). *Social foundations of thought and action.* Engelwood Cliffs, NJ: Prentice-Hall.

75. Brown, J., Halpern, C., & L'Engle, K. (2005). Mass media: a sexual super peer for early maturing girls. *Journal of Adolescent Health, 36,* 420–427.

76. Collins, R. L. (2005). Sex on television and its impact on American Youth: Background and results from Television and Adolescent Sexuality Study. *Child and Adolescent Psychiatric Clinics of North American,* 14, 37-379. Martino, S. C., Collins, R., Elliott, M., Strachman, A, Kanouse, D, & Berry S. (2008).

Exposure to degrading verse nondegrading music lyrics and sexual behavior among youth. *Pediatrics*, 118 (2), 430-441.

77. Kaiser Family Foundation. (2005). *Sex on TV 4, Executive Summary*. Available on-line at www.kff.org or from the Henry J. Kaiser Family Foundation in Menlo Park, CA.

78. Boies, S., Knudson, G., & Young, J. (2004). The internet, sex, and youths: Implication for sexual development. *Sexual Addiction & Complusivity, 11*, 343–363. Kunkel, D., Cope K., Farinola, W., Biedly, R., Rollins, E., & Donnerstein, E. (1999). *Sex on TV: A biennial report to the Kaiser Family Foundation*. Menlo Park, CA: Henry J. Kaiser Family Foundation. Minow, N. N., & LaMay, C. L. (1995). *Abandoned in the wasteland: children, television and the first amendment.*, NY: Hill and Wang.

79. Rand Corporation. (2005). *Does watching sex on television influence teen's sexual activity*. Available on-line at www.rand.org.

80. Capsuto, S. (2000). *Alternate channels: the uncensored story of gay and lesbian images on radio and television*. New York, NY: Ballantine Books.

81. Levine, J. (2002). Harmful to minors: *The perils of protecting our children from sex*. Minneapolis, MN: University of Minnesota Press. Reisman, J. A. (2001/2002). Crafting the homosexual movement. *Regent University Law Review*, 14 (2), 283–342.

82. Paul, J. P., Catania, J., Pollack, L., & Stall, R. (2001). Understanding childhood sexual abuse as a predictor of sexual risk-taking among men who have sex with men: The Urban Men's Health Study. *Child Abuse & Neglect, 25*, 557–584. Tomeo, E., Templer, D. I., Anderson, S., & Kotler, D. (2001) Comparative data of childhood and adolescence molestation in heterosexual and homosexual persons. *Archives of Sexual Behavior, 30*, 535–541.

83. Grundlach, R. (1977). Sexual molestation and rape reported by homosexual and heterosexual women. *Journal of Homosexuality, 2*, 367–384.

84. Doll, L. S., Joy, D., Bartholow, B. N., Bolan, G., Douglas, J. M., Saltzman, L. E., Moss, P. M., & Delgato, W. (1992). Self-reported childhood and adolescent sexual abuse among adult homosexual /bisexual men. *Child Abuse and Neglect*, 16, 855–864.

85. Bradford, J., Ryan, C., & Rothblum, E. D. (1994). National lesbian health care survey: Implications for mental health care. *Journal of Consulting and Clinical Psychology*, 62, 228–242.

86. Simari, C. G., & Baskin, D. (1982). Incestuous experiences within homosexual populations: A preliminary study. *Archives of Sexual Behavior, 11*, 329–344.

87. Finkelhor, D. (1994). Current information on the scope and nature of child sexual abuse. *The Future of Children*, 4, 31–53. Ammerman, R. T., & Hersne, M. (1999). *Assessment of family violence*. NY: John Wiley.

88. Holmes, W., & Slap, G. (1998). Sexual abuse of boys. *Journal of the American Medical Association, 280*, 183-188.

89. Rekers, G. A. (1999). The development of a homosexual orientation. In C. Wolfe (Ed.), Homosexuality *and American public life*, pp. 62–64. Dallas, TX: Spence Publishing Company.

90. Roesler, T., & Deishner, R. W. (1972). Youthful male homosexuality: Homosexual experiences and the process of developing homosexual identity in males age 16 to 22 years. *Journal of the American Medical Association*, 219, 1018–1023.

91. Shrier, D., & Johnson, R. L. (1988). Sexual victimization of boys: An ongoing study of an adolescent medicine clinic population, *Journal of the National Medical Association, 80*, 1189–1193.

92. Louganis, G. & Marcus, E. (1995). *Breaking thee Surface.* New York: Random House, p. 79-80.

93. Tomeo, E., Templer, D. I., Anderson, S., & Kotler, D. (2001) Comparative data of childhood and adolescence molestation in heterosexual and homosexual persons. *Archives of Sexual Behavior, 30*, 60.

94. Downey J. I., & Friedman, R. C. (1998). Female homosexuality: Classical psychoanalytic theory reconsidered. *Journal of the American Psychoanalytic Association*, 46, 471–506. LeVay. S. (1996). *Queer science, p.*143–145. Cambridge, MA: Massachusetts Institute of Technology Press. Whisman, V. (1996). *Queer by choice*. New York, NY: Routledge.

95. Dahir, M. (2001). Why are we gay? *The Advocate*, July 17, pp. 30–42.

96. Vreeland, C. N., & Gallagher, B. J. (1995). The beliefs of members of the American Psychiatric Association on the etiology of male homosexuality: A national survey. *Journal of Psychology*, 129, 507–518.

97. Bem, D. (1996). Exotic becomes erotic: A developmental theory of sexual orientation. *Psychological Review*, 103, 320–335.

98. Miracle, T. S., Miracle A. W., & Baumeister, R. F. (2003). *Human sexuality meeting your basic needs*, p. 331. Upper Saddle River, NJ: Prentice Hall.

99. Stein, E. (1999). *The mismeasure of desire: The science, theory, and ethics of sexual orientation, p. 273*. NY: Oxford University Press.

100. Bailey, J. M., & Zucker, K. J. (1995). Childhood sex-typed behavior and sexual orientation: A conceptual analysis and quantitative review. *Developmental Psychology, 31*, 43–55.

101. Altemeyer, B. (2001). Changes in attitudes toward homosexuals. *Journal of Homosexuality, 42*, 63–75.

102. Medinger, A. (2000). *Growth into manhood, p.21*. Colorado Spring, CO: WaterBrook Press.

103. LeVay. S. (1996). *Queer science, p. 282.* Cambridge, MA: Massachusetts Institute of Technology Press.

CHAPTER 4

1. Byne W., & Parsons, B. (1993). Human sexual orientation: The biological theories reappraised. *Archives of General Psychiatry,* 50, 231-236.

2. Diamond, M. C. (1998). *Enriching heredity: the impact of environment on anatomy of the brain, p. 67.* New York, NY: The Free Press.

3. Burr, W. R., Day, R. W., & Bahr, K. S. (1993). *Family science, p. 46.* Pacific Grove, CA: Brooks/Cole Publishing.

4. Warner, C. T. (2001). *Bonds that make us free.* Salt Lake City, UT: Deseret Book.

5. Frankl, V. (1985). *Man's search for meaning, pp. 86–87.* New York, NY: Pocket Books.

6. Paglia, C.(1994). *Vamps and tramps, pp. 72–73.* New York: Vintage Books.

7. Glock, C. Y. (2004). *Accounting for behavior scientifically and in everyday life.* Unpublished paper available from the author at 319 South Fourth Avenue, Sandpoint, ID 83864.

8. Burr, W. R., Day, R. W., & Bahr, K. S. (1993). *Family science, p. 46.* Pacific Grove, CA: Brooks/Cole Publishing. Werner, E. E., & Smith, R. S. (1992). *Overcoming the odds: High-risk children from birth to adulthood.* Ithaca, NY: Cornell University Press.

9. Williams, R. (2004). Agency: philosophical and spiritual foundations for applied psychology. In A. Jackson and L. Fischer (Ed.), *Turning Freud upside down. Gospel perspective on psychotherapy's fundamental problems.* Provo, UT: Brigham Young University Press.

10. Needleman, J. (2004). National Public Radio program, Morning Edition, 23 February, 2004. See also J. Needleman's, *The American Soul: Rediscovering the wisdom of the founders.* New York, NY: Tarcher/Putnam Press.

11. Smith, H. (2001). *Why religion matters.* San Francisco, CA: Harper Collins.

12. Needleman, J. (2004). National Public Radio program, Morning Edition, 23 February, 2004. See also J. Needleman's, *The American Soul: Rediscovering the wisdom of the founders.* New York, NY: Tarcher/Putnam Press.

13. Bergin, A. E. (2002). *Eternal values, personal growth: A guide on your journey to spiritual, emotional, and social wellness, p. 206.* Provo, UT: Brigham Young University Studies.

14. Fischer, L. (2004). The nature of law: universal but not uniform. In A. Jackson and L. Fischer (Ed.), *Turning Freud upside down. Gospel perspective on psychotherapy's fundamental problems.* Provo, UT: Brigham Young University Press.

15. Holland, J. R. (2007). Helping Those with Same-Gender Attraction, *The Ensign*, October 2007, pp. 42–45.

16. Bergin, A. E. (2002). *Eternal values, personal growth: A guide on your journey to spiritual, emotional, and social wellness.* Provo, UT: Brigham Young University Studies. Fischer, L. (2004). The nature of law: universal but not uniform. In A. Jackson and L. Fischer (Ed.), *Turning Freud upside down. Gospel perspective on psychotherapy's fundamental problems.* Provo, UT: Brigham Young University Press.

17. Nicolosi, J. (1991). *Reparative therapy of male homosexuality: A new clinical approach.* Northvale, NJ: Jason Aronson, Inc.

18. Davies, B., & Rentzer, L. (1994). *Coming out of homosexuality: New freedom for men and women.* P. 20. Westmont, IL: InterVarsity Press.

19. Dawson G., & Fischer, K. W. (1994). *Human behavior and the developing brain.* New York, NY: Guilford Pres. Diamond, M. C. (1998). *Enriching heredity: the impact of environment on anatomy of the brain.* New York, NY: The Free Press. Greenough, W. T., Black, J. E., & Wallace, C. (1987). Experience and brain development, *Child Development, 58*, 539–559. Shore, R. (1997). *Rethinking the brain: New insights into early development.* New York, NY: Families and Work Institute.

20. Breedlove, S. M. (1997). Sex on the brain. *Nature, 389,* 801-805. Kandel, R. R., Schwartz, J., & Jessell, T. (1991). *Principles of neural science.* NY: Elsevier.

21. Greenough, W. T., Black, J. E., & Wallace, C. (1987). Experience and brain development. *Child Development, 58,* 548.

22. Greenough, W. T., Black, J. E., & Wallace, C. (1987). Experience and brain development. *Child Development, 58,* 550.

23. Valenstein, E. S. (1998). *Blaming the brain: The truth about drugs and mental health.* New York, NY: The Free Press. 126–128.

24. Satinover, J. (1996). *Homosexuality and the politics of truth.* Grand Rapids, MI: Baker Books.

25. Bart, P. (1993). Protean woman: The liquidity of female sexuality and the tenacity of lesbian identity. In W. Wilkinson and C. Kitzinger (Eds.), *Heterosexuality: A feminism and psychology reader, pp.* 246–252. London, UK: Sage. Golden, C. (1994). Our politics, our choices: The feminist movement and sexual orientation . In B. Greene and G. Herek (Eds.), *Lesbian and gay psychology: Theory, research and clinical applications, pp. 54–70.* Thousand Oaks, CA: Sage Publications.

26. Lever, J. (1995). Lesbian sex survey: The 1995 Advocate survey of sexuality and relationships: The women. *The Advocate,* August 22, 22–30.

27. Kirkpatrick, M. (1987). Clinical implications of lesbian mother studies. *Journal of Homosexuality, 14,* 202-207.

28. Rosik, C. H. (2003). Motivational, ethical, and epistemological foundations in the treatment of unwanted homoerotic attraction. *Journal of Marital and Family Therapy, 29,* 17-23.

29. Fine, R. (1987). Psychoanalytic theory. In L. Diamant (Ed.), *Male and female homosexuality, pp. 81–95.* New York, NY: Hemisphere Publishing.

30. Throckmorton, W. (2003). Gay-to-straight research published in APA journal. Retrieved online, 9 April 2007, from <www.narth.com/docs/throkarticle.html>.

31. MacIntosh, H. (1995). Attitudes and experiences of Psychoanalysts in analyzing homosexual patients. *Journal of the American Psychoanalytic Association, 42,* 1183–1207.

32. Nicolosi, J., Byrd, A. D., & Potts, R. W. (2000). Retrospective self-reports of changes in homosexual orientation: A consumer survey of conversion therapy clients. *Psychological Reports, 86,* 1071–1088.

33. Robinson, J. W. (1998). *Understanding the meaning of change for married Latter-day Saint men with histories of homosexual activity, pp.* 319–320. Unpublished doctoral dissertation, Brigham Young University, Provo, Utah.

34. Nicolosi, J., & Nicolosi, L. A. (2002). *A parent's guide to preventing homosexuality, pp.* 140–141. Downers Grove, IL: InterVarsity Press.

35. Spitzer, R. L. (2003). Can some gay men and lesbians change their sexual orientation? 200 participants reporting a change from homosexual to heterosexual orientation. *Archives of Sexual Behavior, 32(5),* 403–417.

36. Herschberger, S. (2003). Guttman Scalability Confirms the Effectiveness of Reparative Therapy. *Archives of Sexual Behavior, 32(5),* 438-444.

37. Nicolosi, J. (1991). *Reparative therapy of male homosexuality: A new clinical approach.* Northvale, NJ: Jason Aronson, Inc. Satinover, J. (1996). *Homosexuality and the politics of truth.* Grand Rapids, MI: Baker Books. van den Aardweg, G. (1985). *Homosexuality and hope: A psychologist talks about treatment and change.* Ann Arbor, MI: Servant Books.

38. Cohen, R. (2001*). Coming out straight: Understanding and healing homosexuality.* Winchester, VA: Oakhill Press.

39. Anderson, N. T. (1998). *A way of escape.* Eugene, OR: Harvest House Press. Davies, B., & Rentzer, L. (1994). *Coming out of homosexuality: New freedom for men and women.* Westmont, IL: InterVarsity Press.

40. Bieber, I. (1976). A discussion of homosexuality: The ethical challenge. *Journal of Consulting and Clinical Psychology, 44,* 163–166. Davies, B., & Gilbert, L. *(2001). Portraits of freedom: 14 people who came out of homosexuality.* Downers Grove, IL: InterVarsity Press. Nicolosi, J. (1993). *Healing homosexuality: Case stories of reparative therapy.* Northvale, NJ: Jason Aronson, Inc. Satinover,

J. (1996). *Homosexuality and the politics of truth*. Grand Rapids, MI: Baker Books.

41. Stein, E. (1999). *The mismeasure of desire: The science, theory, and ethics of sexual orientation*. New York, NY: Oxford University Press.

42. Stein, E. (1999). *The mismeasure of desire: The science, theory, and ethics of sexual orientation, p.260*. New York, NY: Oxford University Press.

43. Stein, E. (1999). *The mismeasure of desire: The science, theory, and ethics of sexual orientation*, p. 261. New York, NY: Oxford University Press.

44. Dailey, T. J. (2003). *Dark obsession: the tragedy and threat of the homosexual lifestyle, p. 126*. Nashville, TN: Broadman & Holman Publishers.

45. Jones, S. L., & Yarhouse, M. A. (2007). Ex-gays: a longitudinal study of religiously mediate change in sexual orientation. Downers Grove, IL: InterVarsity Press.

46. Andersen, S., & Andersen, K. (1998). *Homosexuality: Symptoms and free agency*. Springville, UT: Bonneville Books.

CHAPTER 5

1. King, B. M. (2004). *Human sexuality today, p. 178*. Upper Saddle River, NJ: Prentice Hall.

2. Schmidt, T. (1995). *Straight and narrow? p. 154*. Downer Grove, IL: InterVarsity Press.

3. Nicolosi, J. (1993). *Healing homosexuality: Case stories of reparative therapy, pp. 35–36*. Northvale, NJ: Jason Aronson, Inc.

4. Medinger, A. (2000). *Growth into manhood*. Colorado Spring, CO: WaterBrook Press.

CHAPTER 6

1. Medinger, A. (2000). *Growth into manhood*. Colorado Spring, CO: WaterBrook Press.

2. Davies, B., & Rentzer, L. (1994). *Coming out of homosexuality: New freedom for men and women*. Westmont, IL: InterVarsity Press. Medinger, A. (2000). *Growth into manhood*. Colorado Spring, CO: WaterBrook Press. Murphy, T. F. (1992). Redirecting sexual orientation: Techniques and justifications. *Journal of Sex Research, 29*, 501–523. Park, J. (1997). *Resolving homosexual problems: A guide for LDS men*. Salt Lake City, UT: Century Publishing. Nicolosi, J. (1991). *Reparative therapy of male homosexuality: A new clinical approach*. Northvale, NJ: Jason Aronson, Inc. Socarides, C. (1995). *Homosexuality: A freedom too far*. Phoenix, AZ: Adam Margrave. van den Aardweg, G. (1985). *Homosexuality and hope: A psychologist talks about treatment and change*. Ann Arbor, MI: Servant Books. Zucker, K. J., & Bradley, S. J. (1995). *Gender iden-*

tity disorder and psychosexual problems in children and adolescents. New York, NY: Guilford Press.

3. Fitzgibbons, R. (1999). The origins and therapy of homosexual attraction disorder. In C. Wolfe (Ed.), *Homosexuality and American public life*, pp. 85–97. Dallas, TX: Spence. Nicolosi, J. (1991). *Reparative therapy of male homosexuality: A new clinical approach.* Northvale, NJ: Jason Aronson, Inc.

4. Nicolosi, J., & Nicolosi, L. A. (2002). *A parent's guide to preventing homosexuality.* Downers Grove, IL: InterVarsity Press. 30. Bieber, I., & Bieber, T. (1979). Male homosexuality. *Canadian Journal of Psychiatry*, 24, 411-415.

5. Bieber, I., & Bieber, T. (1979). Male homosexuality. *Canadian Journal of Psychiatry*, 24, 409–421.

6. Bieber, I. (1976). A discussion of homosexuality: The ethical challenge. *Journal of Consulting and Clinical Psychology*, *44,* 165.

7. Fitzgibbons, R. (1999). The origins and therapy of homosexual attraction disorder. In C. Wolfe (Ed.), *Homosexuality and American public life*, pp. 85–97. Dallas, TX: Spence.

8. Medinger, A. (2000). *Growth into manhood.* Colorado Spring, CO: Water-Brook Press.

9. Bailey, J. M., & Zucker, K. J. (1995). Childhood sex-typed behavior and sexual orientation: A conceptual analysis and quantitative review. *Developmental Psychology, 31,* 43–55.

10. Medinger, A. (2000). *Growth into manhood*, p. 248. Colorado Spring, CO: WaterBrook Press.

11. Nicolosi, J., & Nicolosi, L. A. (2002). *A parent's guide to preventing homosexuality, p. 32.* Downers Grove, IL: InterVarsity Press.

12. Lauer, R., & Lauer, J. (1991). The long-term relational consquences of problematic family backgrounds. *Family Relations, 40,* 377–384.

13. Howard, J. (2001). *Out of Egypt: One woman's journey out of lesbianism, p. 106.* Grand Rapids, MI: Kregel Publications.

14. Socarides, C. (1995). *Homosexuality: A freedom too far.* Phoenix, AZ: Adam Margrave.

15. Nicolosi, J., & Nicolosi, L. A. (2002). *A parent's guide to preventing homosexuality*, p. 75. Downers Grove, IL: InterVarsity Press.

16. Worthen, A., & Davies, B. (1996). *Someone I love is gay: how family and friends can respond, p. 128.* Downers Grove, IL: InterVarsity Press.

17. Worthen, A., & Davies, B. (1996). *Someone I love is gay: how family and friends can respond, p. 129.* Downers Grove, IL: InterVarsity Press.

18. Nicolosi, J., & Nicolosi, L. A. (2002). *A parent's guide to preventing homosexuality.* Downers Grove, IL: InterVarsity Press.

19. Byrd, A.D. & Byrd, K.M. (2007). Dual-Gender parenting: a social science perspective for optimal child rearing in Lynn D. Wardle and Camille Williams (Eds.), *Family Law: Balancing Interests and Pursuing Priorities*, pp. 382–390. Buffalo, New York: William S. Hein & Company.

20. Diamond, L. M. (2005). A new view of lesbian subtypes. *Psychology of Women Quarterly, 29*(2), 119-128.

21. Socarides, C. (1995). *Homosexuality: A freedom too far.* Phoenix, AZ: Adam Margrave.

22. Rekers, G., & Kilgus, M. (2001/2002). Studies of homosexual parenting: A critical review. *Regent University Law Review, 14* (2), 53.

23. Howard, J. (2001). *Out of Egypt: One woman's journey out of lesbianism, p. 111.* Grand Rapids, MI: Kregel Publications.

24. Nicolosi, J., & Nicolosi, L. A. (2002). *A parent's guide to preventing homosexuality, p.* 95. Downers Grove, IL: InterVarsity Press.

25. Kaiser Family Foundation. (2005). *Sex on TV 4, Executive Summary.* Available on-line at www.kff.org or from the Henry J. Kaiser Family Foundation in Menlo Park, CA. Steinberg, L. (2007). Adolescence. New York: McGraw-Hill.

26. Byrd, A.D. & Cox, S.E. (2007). Strict scrutiny of prospective adoptive parents: what children really need. In A. Scott Loveless & Thomas B. Holman (Ed.), *The Family In The New Millennium*, pp. 204–219. Westpoint, Connecticut: Praeger,.

27. Dobson, J. (2001). *Bringing up boys, p. 123.* Carol Stream, IL: Tyndale House Publishers.

28. Regnerus, M. D. (2007). *Forbidden fruit: Sex & religion in the lives of American teenagers.* New York: Oxford University Press.

29. Rekers, G. A. (1982). *Shaping your child's sexual identity, p. 29.* Grand Rapids, MI: Baker Book House.

30. Barlow, B. (1995). *Worth waiting for: Sexual abstinence before marriage.* Salt Lake City, UT: Deseret Book. St. James, R. (1997). *Wait for me: The beauty of sexual purity.* Nashville, TN: Thomas Nelson Publisher.

31. Erikson, E. H. (1968). *Identity, youth, and crisis.* New York, NY: Norton.

32. Feldman, R. S. (2003). *Development across the life span, p.* 420. Upper Saddle River, NJ: Prentice Hall.

33. Berk, L. E. (2001). *Development through the lifespan*, p. 390. Boston, MA: Allyn and Bacon.

34. Marcia, J. E. (1980). Identity in adolescence. In J. Adelson (Ed.), *Handbook of adolescent psychology*, pp. 159–187. New York, NY: Wiley & Sons.

35. Rekers, G. A. (1982). *Shaping your child's sexual identity, p.* 21. Grand Rapids, MI: Baker Book House.

36. Mitchel, K., & Sugar, M. (2003). Foster child concerned with orientation. Annie's Mailbox (advice column), Lincoln Journal Star, Friday, April 18, p. 5D.

37. Ryan, C., & Futterman, D. (1998). *Lesbian & Gay youth: Care & counseling.* New York, NY: Columbia University Press.

38. *Just the facts about sexual orientation & youth: A primer for principles, educators and school personnel.* (1999). Washington, DC: The American Psychological Association.

39. Shidlo, A. (2002). Changing sexual orientation: A consumers' report. *Professional Psychology: Research & Practice, 33,* 249–259. Stein, T. S. (1996). A critique of approaches to changing sexual orientation. In R. P. Cabaj and T. S. Stein (Eds.), *Textbook of homosexuality and mental health, pp. 525–537.* Washington, DC: American Psychiatric Press.

40. Packard, B. (2000). Ye are the temples of God. *Ensign,* Nov. 2000, p. 72-74.

41. Dailey, T. J. (2003). *Dark obsession: the tragedy and threat of the homosexual lifestyle, p. 127.* Nashville, TN: Broadman & Holman Publishers.

42. Nicolosi, J., & Nicolosi, L. A. (2002). *A parent's guide to preventing homosexuality, p.* 44–45. Downers Grove, IL: InterVarsity Press.

43. Rekers, G. A., & Mead, S. (1979). Early intervention for female sexual identity disturbance: Self-monitoring of play behavior. *Journal of Abnormal Child Psychology, 7,* 402-409.

44. Drescher, J. (1998). Contemporary psychoanalytic psychotherapy with gay men: With a commentary on reparative therapy of homosexuality. *Journal of Gay and Lesbian Psychotherapy, 2,* 51–74. Martin, A. D. (1984). The emperor's new clothes: Modern attempts to change sexual orientation. In E. S. Hetrich and T. S. Stein (Eds.), *Psychotherapy with homosexuals, pp. 23–58.* Washington, DC: American Psychiatric Press.

45. Davision, G. C. (2001). Conceptual and ethical issues in therapy for the psychological problems of gay men, lesbians and bisexuals. *Journal of Clinical Psychology, 57,* 659–704. Garnets, L., Hancock, K. A., Cochran, S. D., Goodchilds, J., & Peplau, L. A. (1991). Issues in psychotherapy with lesbians and gay men: A survey of psychologists. *American Psychologist, 46,* 964–972. Halderman, D. C. (1994). The practice and ethics of sexual orientation conversion therapy. *Journal of Consulting and Clinical Psychology, 62,* 221–227. Tozer, E. E., & McClanahan, M. K. (1999). Treating the purple menace: Ethical consideration of conversion therapy and affirmative alternatives. *Counseling Psychologist, 27,* 722–742.

46. Stein, T. S. (1996). A critique of approaches to changing sexual orientation. In R. P. Cabaj and T. S. Stein (Eds.), *Textbook of homosexuality and mental health*. p. 535.Washington, DC: American Psychiatric Press.

47. Green, R. (1987). *The sissy boy syndrome*: New Haven: Yale University Press.

48. Rosik, C. H. (2003). Motivational, ethical, and epistemological foundations in the treatment of unwanted homoerotic attraction. *Journal of Marital and Family Therapy, 29*, 14.

49. Yarhouse, M. & Nowacki, S. (2007). The many meanings of marriage: divergent perspectives seeking common ground. *The Family Journal, 15,* 73.

50. Nicolosi, J., & Nicolosi, L. A. (2002). *A parent's guide to preventing homosexuality*. Downers Grove, IL: InterVarsity Press. Socarides, C. (1995). *Homosexuality: A freedom too far*. Phoenix, AZ: Adam Margrave.

CHAPTER 7

1. Yarhouse, M. & Nowacki, S. (2007). The many meanings of marriage: divergent perspectives seeking common ground. *The Family Journal, 15,* 36–45.

2. Bieschke, K., Perez, R., DeBord, K. (2007). *Handbook of counseling and psychotherapy with lesbian, gay, bisexual, and transgender clients (2nd Edition)*. Washington, DC: American Psychological Association.

3. Bruce, T. (2001). *The new thought police: Inside the left's assault on free speech and free minds*. Roseville, CA: Prima Publishing.

4. Sullivan, M. (2003). *Sexual minorities: discrimination, challenges and development in America*. New York: Haworth Press.

5. Eisenberg, M., & Resnick, M. (2006). Suicidality among gay lesbian, and bisexual youth: There role of protective factors. *Journal of Adolescent Health, 39,* 662–668. Swigonski, M. E., Ward, K, & Mama, R. (2001). *From hate crimes to human rights: A tribute to Matthew Shepard*. Binghamton, NY: Haworth Press.

6. Swidler, A. (1993). *Homosexuality and world religions*. Valley Forge, PA: Trinity Press.

7. Rekers, G. A. (1982). *Shaping your child's sexual identity, p.* 51. Grand Rapids, MI: Baker Book House.

8. Kirk, M., & Madsen, H. (1989). *After the ball: How American will conquer its fear and hated of gays in the 90's*. New York, NY: Doubleday. Reisman, J. A. (2001/2002). Crafting hi/homosexual movement. *Regent University Law Review,* 14 (2), 283–342. Rondeau, P. E. (2001/2002). Selling homosexuality to America. *Regent University Law Review, 14* (2), 443–486.

9. Redding, R. E. (2001). Sociopolitical diversity in psychology: The case for pluralism. *American Psychologist, 56,* 205–215.

10. Wright, R. & Cummings, N. Eds. (2005) *Destructive trends in mental health*. New York, NY: Routledge.

11. Baldwin, S. (2001/2002). Child molestation and the homosexual movement. *Regent University Law Review*, 14 (2), 267–282. Gordon. S., & Cohen, V. (2000). *All families are different*. Amherst, NY: Prometheus Books. Greenberg, K. E., & Halebian, C. (1996). *Zack's story*. (1996). Minneapolis, MN: Lerner Publishing. Hart, J. (1998). *Gay sex: A manual for men who love men*. Los Angeles, CA: Alyson Publishing. Newman, L., & Souza, D. (2000). *Heather has two mommies*. Los Angels, CA: Alyson Publishing.

12. Stacey, J. (2007. Gay and lesbian families: Queer like us. In A. Skolnick, & J. Skolnick (Eds.), *Family in Transition* 14ᵗʰ Edition, pp. 448–469. Boston, MA: Allyn & Bacon.

13. Bennett, W. H. (2003). *The broken hearth: Reversing the moral collapse of the American family*. Anderson, IN: Broadway Press.

14. Ferrara, F. (2002). *Childhood sexual abuse: Developmental effects across the lifespan*. Belmont, CA: Thomson/Wadsworth. Johnson, J. L., & Grant, G. (2007). *Casebook: Sexual abuse*. Boston, MA: Allyn & Bacon.

15. Socarides, C. (1995). *Homosexuality: A freedom too far, pp.* 13–14. Phoenix, AZ: Adam Margrave.

16. Bruce, T. (2001). *The new thought police: Inside the left's assault on free speech and free minds, p.* xix. Roseville, CA: Prima Publishing.

17. Reisman, J. A. (2001/2002). Crafting the homosexual movement. *Regent University Law Review*, 14 (2), 283–342.

18. Bergner, M. (1995). *Setting love in order*: Hope and healing for the homosexual. Grand Rapids, MI: Baker Books. Byrd, A.D. (1993). Interview: An LDS reparative therapy approach for male homosexuality. *Association of Mormon Counselors and Psychotherapists, 19*, 90–104.

19. Davies, B., & Gilbert, L. *(2001). Portraits of freedom: 14 people who came out of homosexuality*. Downers Grove, IL: InterVarsity Press. Eldridge, E. (1995). *Born that way: A true story of overcoming homosexual attraction with insights for friends, families, and leaders*. Salt Lake City, UT: Deseret Book.

20. Dailey, T. J. (2003). *Dark obsession: the tragedy and threat of the homosexual lifestyle, p.* 137. Nashville, TN: Broadman & Holman Publishers.

21. Howard, J. (2001). *Out of Egypt: One woman's journey out of lesbianism, p.* 257-259. Grand Rapids, MI: Kregel Publications.

22. Anonymous. (2002). My battle with homosexual attraction, p. 49. *The Ensign*, August.

23. Anonymous. (2002). My battle with homosexual attraction, pp. 49–51. *The Ensign*, August.

24. Rekers, G. A. (1982). *Shaping your child's sexual identity.* Grand Rapids, MI: Baker Book House.

25. Fitzgibbons, R. (1999). The origins and therapy of homosexual attraction disorder. In C. Wolfe (Ed.), *Homosexuality and American public life*, pp. 85–97. Dallas, TX: Spence.

26. Fitzgibbons, R. (1999). The origins and therapy of homosexual attraction disorder. In C. Wolfe (Ed.), *Homosexuality and American public life*, pp. 85–97. Dallas, TX: Spence.

27. Nicolosi, J., & Nicolosi, L. A. (2002). *A parent's guide to preventing homosexuality.* Downers Grove, IL: InterVarsity Press. 173. Wolfe, C. (1999). Preface. In C. Wolfe (Ed.), *Homosexuality and American public life*, pp. ix-xiv. Dallas, TX: Spence Publishing.

28. Fergusson, D., Horwood, L, & Beautrais, A. (1999). Is sexual orientation related to mental health problems and suicidality in young people? *Archives of General Psychiatry, 56*, 876–880. Remafedi, G., French, S., Story, M., Resnick, M., & Blum, R. (1998). The relationship between suicide risk and sexual orientation: Results of a population-based study. *American Journal of Public Health, 88*, 57–60. Sandfort, T., de Graaf, R., Biji, R., & Schnabel, M. (2001). Same-sex sexual behavior and psychiatric disorders. *Archives of General Psychiatry, 58*, 85-91.

29. Sandfort, T., de Graaf, R., Bijl, R., & Schnabel, P. (2001). Same-sex behavior and psychiatric disorders. *Archives of General Psychiatry, 58*, 85-91. Frisch, M., & Hviid, A. (2006). Childhood family correlates of heterosexual and homosexual marriages: A national cohort study of two million Danes. *Archives of Sexual Behavior, 35*, 533-547. For an opposing opinion see Meyer, I. H. (2003). Prejudice, social stress, and mental health in lesbian, gay, and bisexual populations. *Psychological Bulletin, 129* (5), 674-697. Also see Cochran, S., Sullivan, J., & Mays, V. (2003). Prevalence of mental disorders, psychological distress, and mental service use among lesbian, gay, and bisexual adults in the United States. *Journal of Consulting and Clinical Psychology, 71*(1), 53-61.

30. Whitehead, N., & Whitehead, B. (1999). *My genes made me do it.* Lafayette, Louisiana: Huntington House Press.

31. American Psychological Association. (2008). Answers to your questions: for a better understanding of sexual orientation and homosexuality, p. 2. Retrieved on-line July 1, 2008 from: http://www. apa.org/topics/sorientation.pdf

32. Dalton, E. S. (2007). Stay on the path. *Ensign* (magazine), May, pages 112-114.

ABOUT
DOUGLAS A. ABBOTT

Douglas A. Abbott is currently a professor of Child, Youth & Family Studies at the University of Nebraska in Lincoln Nebraska where he has been teaching and doing research for 25 years. He received a bachelor's degree in human biology from Oregon State University in 1974, a master's degree in child development from Brigham Young University in 1979, and a doctorate in Child & Family Studies from the University of Georgia in 1983.

For the past five years he has been studying adolescent sexual decision making with a special emphasis on teens to choose sexual abstinence. During this project he unexpectedly encountered a few teens that were confused and concerned about their sexual orientation. This book is a result of his investigation of this phenomenon.

Dr. Abbott's other focus has been cross-cultural research on families enduring traumatic events such as extreme poverty in India and the violent death of a child in Israel. He completed a U.S. Fulbright Scholar Award to India in 1996 and to Israel and Palestine in 2006. In 2000-2001 he taught full-time at Zayed University in the United Arab Emirates at an all women's Muslim college. He has studied the religion of Islam for many years and currently teaches a course on Islam and Muslim families at the University of Nebraska. He is a practicing Christian with a special interest in the influence of religion on family health and well-being.

About
A. Dean Byrd

A. Dean Byrd, PhD, MBA, MPH is the President of the Thrasher Research Fund and a member of the University of Utah School of Medicine faculty with appointments in the Department of Family and Preventive Medicine and in the Department of Psychiatry. In addition, he is Adjunct Professor in the Department of Family Studies, also at the University of Utah. Dr. Byrd received his academic training at Spartanburg Methodist College, Brigham Young University, Virginia Commonwealth University and Medical College of Virginia, Loyola University and the University of Utah. Dr. Byrd is the author of five books and more than two hundred total peer-reviewed journal articles (in mental health as well as law journals), book chapters, book reviews, and opinion editorials on homosexuality, homosexual marriage, adoption by homosexual couples, and other family related topics. As a licensed clinical psychologist, he has served as an expert witness in court proceedings on family related issues in the United States and abroad.